# *Theodore Roosevelt and His Times*

## *Harold Howland*

# Contents

# THEODORE ROOSEVELT AND HIS TIMES

BY

Harold Howland

# CHAPTER I. THE YOUNG FIGHTER

There is a line of Browning's that should stand as epitaph for Theodore Roosevelt: "I WAS EVER A FIGHTER." That was the essence of the man, that the keynote of his career. He met everything in life with a challenge. If it was righteous, he fought for it; if it was evil, he hurled the full weight of his finality against it. He never capitulated, never sidestepped, never fought foul. He carried the fight to the enemy.

His first fight was for health and bodily vigor. It began, at the age of nine. Physically he was a weakling, his thin and ill-developed body racked with asthma. But it was only the physical power that was wanting, never the intellectual or the spiritual. He owed to his father, the first Theodore, the wise counsel that launched him on his determined contest against ill health. On the third floor of the house on East Twentieth Street in New York where he was born, October 27, 1858, his father had constructed an outdoor gymnasium, fitted with all the usual paraphernalia. It was an impressive moment, Roosevelt used to say in later years, when his father first led him into that gymnasium and said to him, "Theodore, you have the brains, but brains are of comparatively little use without the body; you have got to make your body, and it lies with you to make it. It's dull, hard work, but you can do it." The boy knew that his father was right; and he set those white, powerful teeth of his and took up the drudgery of daily, monotonous exercise with bars and rings and weights. "I can see him now," says his sister, "faithfully going through various exercises, at different times of the day, to broaden the chest narrowed by this terrible shortness of breath, to make the limbs and back strong, and able to bear the weight of what was coming to him later in life."

All through his boyhood the young Theodore Roosevelt kept up his fight for strength. He was too delicate to attend school, and was taught by private tutors.

He spent many of his summers, and sometimes some of the winter months, in the woods of Maine. These outings he thoroughly enjoyed, but it is certain that the main motive which sent him into the rough life of the woods to hunt and tramp, to paddle and row and swing an axe, was the obstinate determination to make himself physically fit.

His fight for bodily power went on through his college course at Harvard and during the years that he spent in ranch life in the West. He was always intensely interested in boxing, although he was never of anything like championship caliber in the ring. His first impulse to learn to defend himself with his hands had a characteristic birth.

During one of his periodical attacks of asthma he was sent alone to Moosehead Lake in Maine. On the stagecoach that took him the last stage of the journey he met two boys of about his own age. They quickly found, he says, in his "Autobiography", that he was "a foreordained and predestined victim" for their rough teasing, and they "industriously proceeded to make life miserable" for their fellow traveler. At last young Roosevelt could endure their persecutions no loner, and tried to fight. Great was his discomfiture when he discovered that either of them alone could handle him "with easy contempt." They hurt him little, but, what was doubtless far more humiliating, they prevented him from doing any damage whatever in return.

The experience taught the boy, better than any good advice could have done, that he must learn to defend himself. Since he had little natural prowess, he realized that he must supply its place by training. He secured his father's approval for a course of boxing lessons, upon which he entered at once. He has described himself as a "painfully slow and awkward pupil," who worked for two or three years before he made any perceptible progress.

In college Roosevelt kept at boxing practice. Even in those days no antagonist, no matter how much his superior, ever made him "quit." In his ranching days, that training with his fists stood him in good stead. Those were still primitive days out in the Dakotas, though now, as Roosevelt has said, that land of the West has "'gone, gone with the lost Atlantis,' gone to the isle of ghosts and of strange dead memories." A man needed to be able to take care of himself in that Wild West then. Roosevelt had many stirring experiences but only one that he called "serious trouble."

He was out after lost horses and came to a primitive little hotel, consisting of a bar-room, a dining-room, a lean-to kitchen, and above a loft with fifteen or twenty beds in it. When he entered the bar-room late in the evening--it was a cold night and there was nowhere else to go--a would-be "bad man," with a cocked revolver in each hand, was striding up and down the floor, talking with crude profanity. There were several bullet holes in the clock face, at which he had evidently been shooting. This bully greeted the newcomer as "Four Eyes," in reference to his spectacles, and announced, "Four Eyes is going to treat." Roosevelt joined in the laugh that followed and sat down behind the stove, thinking to escape notice. But the "bad man" followed him, and in spite of Roosevelt's attempt to pass the matter over as a joke, stood over him, with a gun in each hand and using the foulest language. "He was foolish," said Roosevelt, in describing the incident, "to stand so near, and moreover, his heels were closer together, so that his position was unstable." When he repeated his demand that Four Eyes should treat, Roosevelt rose as if to comply. As he rose he struck quick and hard with his right fist just to the left side of the point of the jaw, and, as he straightened up hit with his left, and again with his right. The bully's guns went off, whether intentionally or involuntarily no one ever knew. His head struck the corner of the bar as he fell, and he lay senseless. "When my assailant came to," said Roosevelt, "he went down to the station and left on a freight." It was eminently characteristic of Roosevelt that he tried his best to avoid trouble, but that, when he could not avoid it honorably, he took care to make it "serious trouble" for the other fellow.

Even after he became President, Roosevelt liked to box, until an accident, of which for many years only his intimate friends were aware, convinced him of the unwisdom of the game for a man of his age and optical disabilities. A young artillery captain, with whom he was boxing in the White House, cross-countered him on the left eye, and the blow broke the little blood-vessels. Ever afterward, the sight of that eye was dim; and, as he said, "if it had been the right eye I should have been entirely unable to shoot." To "a mighty hunter before the Lord" like Theodore Roosevelt, such a result would have been a cardinal calamity.

By the time his experiences in the West were over, Roosevelt's fight for health had achieved its purpose. Bill Sewall, the woodsman who had introduced the young Roosevelt to the life of the out-of-doors in Maine, and who afterward went out

West with him to take up the cattle business, offers this testimony: "He went to Dakota a frail young man, suffering from asthma and stomach trouble. When he got back into the world again, he was as husky as almost any man I have ever seen who wasn't dependent on his arms for his livelihood. He weighed one hundred and fifty pounds, and was clear bone, muscle, and grit."

This battle won by the force of sheer determination, the young Roosevelt never ceased fighting. He knew that the man who neglects exercise and training, no matter how perfect his physical trim, is certain to "go back." One day many years afterward on Twenty-third Street, on the way back from an Outlook editorial luncheon, I ran against his shoulder, as one often will with a companion on crowded city streets, and felt as if it were a massive oak tree into which I had bumped. Roosevelt the grown man of hardened physique was certainly a transformation from that "reed shaken with the wind" of his boyhood days.

When Theodore Roosevelt left Harvard in 1880, he plunged promptly into a new fight--in the political arena. He had no need to earn his living; his father had left him enough money to take care of that. But he had no intention or desire to live a life of leisure. He always believed that the first duty of a man was to "pull his own weight in the boat"; and his irrepressible energy demanded an outlet in hard, constructive work. So he took to politics, and as a good Republican ("at that day" he said, "a young man of my bringing up and convictions, could only join the Republican party") he knocked at the door of the Twenty-first District Republican Association in the city of New York. His friends among the New Yorkers of cultivated taste and comfortable life disapproved of his desire to enter this new environment. They told him that politics were "low"; that the political organizations were not run by "gentlemen," and that he would find there saloonkeepers, horse-car conductors, and similar persons, whose methods he would find rough and coarse and unpleasant. Roosevelt merely replied that, if this were the case, it was those men and not his "silk-stocking" friends who constituted the governing class--and that he intended to be one of the governing class himself. If he could not hold his own with those who were really in practical politics, he supposed he would have to quit; but he did not intend to quit without making the experiment.

At every step in his career Theodore Roosevelt made friends. He made them not "unadvisedly or lightly" but with the directness, the warmth, and the permanence that were inseparable from the Roosevelt character. One such friend he acquired at this stage of his progress. In that District Association, from which his friends had warned him away, he found a young Irishman who had been a gang leader in the rough-and-tumble politics of the East Side. Driven by the winter wind of man's ingratitude from Tammany Hall into the ranks of the opposite party, Joe Murray was at this time one of the lesser captains in "the Twenty-first" Roosevelt soon came to like him. He was "by nature as straight a man, as fearless, and as staunchly loyal," said Roosevelt, "as any one whom I have ever met, a man to be trusted in any position demanding courage, integrity, and good faith." The liking was returned by the eager and belligerent young Irishman, though he has confessed that he was first led to consider Roosevelt as a political ally from the point of view of his advantages as a vote-getter.

The year after Roosevelt joined "the governing class" in Morton Hall, "a large barn-like room over a saloon," with furniture "of the canonical kind; dingy benches, spittoons, a dais at one end with a table and chair, and a stout pitcher for iced water, and on the walls pictures of General Grant, and of Levi P. Morton," Joe Murray was engaged in a conflict with "the boss" and wanted a candidate of his own for the Assembly. He picked out Roosevelt, because he thought that with him he would be most likely to win. Win they did; the nomination was snatched away from the boss's man, and election followed. The defeated boss good-humoredly turned in to help elect the young silk-stocking who had been the instrument of his discomfiture.

# CHAPTER II. IN THE NEW YORK ASSEMBLY

Roosevelt was twice reelected to the Assembly, the second time in 1883, a year when a Republican success was an outstanding exception to the general course of events in the State. His career at Albany was marked by a series of fights for decency and honesty. Each new contest showed him a fearless antagonist, a hard hitter, and a man of practical common sense and growing political wisdom. Those were the days of the famous "black horse cavalry" in the New York Legislature--a group of men whose votes could always be counted on by the special interests and those corporations whose managers proceeded on the theory that the way to get the legislation they wanted, or to block the legislation they did not want, was to buy the necessary votes. Perhaps one-third of the members of the Legislature, according to Roosevelt's estimate, were purchasable. Others were timid. Others again were either stupid or honestly so convinced of the importance of "business" to the general welfare that they were blind to corporate faults. But Theodore Roosevelt was neither purchasable, nor timid, nor unable to distinguish between the legitimate requirements of business and its unjustifiable demands. He developed as a natural leader of the honest opposition to the "black horse cavalry."

The situation was complicated by what were known as "strike bills." These were bills which, if passed, might or might not have been in the public interest, but would certainly have been highly embarrassing to the private interests involved. The purpose of their introduction was, of course, to compel the corporations to pay bribes to ensure their defeat. Roosevelt had one interesting and illuminating experience with the "black horse cavalry." He was Chairman of the Committee on Cities. The representatives of one of the great railways brought to him a bill to permit the extension of its terminal facilities in one of the big cities of the State, and asked him to take charge of it. Roosevelt looked into the proposed bill and found that it was a measure that ought to be passed quite as much in the public interest as is the interest of the railroad. He agreed to stand sponsor for the bill, provided he were assured that no money would be used to push it. The assurance was given. When the bill came before his committee for consideration, Roosevelt found that he could not get it reported out either favorably or unfavorably. So he decided to force matters. In accordance with his life-long practice, he went into the decisive committee meeting perfectly sure what he was going to do, and otherwise fully prepared.

There was a broken chair in the room, and when he took his seat a leg of that chair was unobtrusively ready to his hand. He moved that the bill be reported favorably.

The gang, without debate, voted "No." He moved that it be reported unfavorably. Again the gang voted "No." Then he put the bill in his pocket and announced that he proposed to report it anyhow. There was almost a riot. He was warned that his conduct would be exposed on the floor of the Assembly. He replied that in that case he would explain publicly in the Assembly the reasons which made him believe that the rest of the committee were trying, from motives of blackmail, to prevent any report of the bill. The bill was reported without further protest, and the threatened riot did not come off, partly, said Roosevelt, "because of the opportune production of the chair-leg." But the young fighter found that he was no farther along: the bill slumbered soundly on the calendar, and nothing that he could do availed to secure consideration of it. At last the representative of the railroad suggested that some older and more experienced leader might be able to get the bill passed where he had failed. Roosevelt could do nothing but assent. The bill was put in charge of an "old Parliamentary hand," and after a decent lapse of time, went through without opposition. The complete change of heart on the part of the black horsemen under the new leadership was vastly significant. Nothing could be proved; but much could be surmised.

Another incident of Roosevelt's legislative career reveals the bull-dog tenacity of the man. Evidence had been procured that a State judge had been guilty of improper, if not of corrupt, relations with certain corporate interests. This judge had held court in a room of one of the "big business" leaders of that time. He had written in a letter to this financier, "I am willing to go to the very verge of judicial discretion to serve your vast interests." There was strong evidence that he had not stopped at the verge. The blood of the young Roosevelt boiled at the thought of this stain on the judicial ermine. His party elders sought patronizingly to reassure him; but he would have none of it. He rose in the Assembly and demanded the impeachment of the unworthy judge. With perfect candor and the naked vigor that in the years to come was to become known the world around he said precisely what he meant. Under the genial sardonic advice of the veteran Republican leader, who "wished to give young Mr. Roosevelt time to think about the wisdom of his course," the Assembly voted not to take up his "loose charges." It looked like ignominious defeat. But the next day the young firebrand was back to the attack again, and the next day, and the next. For eight days he kept up the fight; each day the reputation of this contest for a forlorn hope grew and spread throughout the State. On the eighth day he demanded that the resolution be voted on again, and the opposition collapsed. Only six votes were cast against his motion. It is true that the investigation ended in a coat of whitewash. But the evidence was so strong that no one could be in doubt that it WAS whitewash. The young legislator, whose party mentors had seen before him nothing but a ruined career, had won a smashing moral victory.

Roosevelt was not only a fighter from his first day in public life to the last, but he was a fighter always against the same evils. Two incidents more than a quarter of a century apart illustrate this fact. A bill was introduced in the Assembly in those earlier days to prohibit the manufacture of cigars in tenement houses in New York City. It was proposed by the Cigar-Makers' Union. Roosevelt was appointed one of a committee of three to investigate the subject. Of the other two members, one did not believe in the bill but confessed privately that he must support it because the labor unions were strong in his district. The other, with equal frankness, confessed that he had to oppose the bill because certain interests who had a strong hold upon him disapproved it, but declared his belief that if Roosevelt would look into the matter he would find that the proposed legislation was good. Politics, and politicians, were like that in those days--as perhaps they still are in these. The young aristocrat, who was fast becoming a stalwart and aggressive democrat, expected to find himself against the bill; for, as he has said, the "respectable people" and the "business men" whom he knew did not believe in such intrusions upon the right even of working-men to do what they would with their own. The laissez faire doctrine of economic life was good form in those days.

But the only member of that committee that approached the question with an open mind found that his first impressions were wrong. He went down into the tenement houses to see for himself. He found cigars being made under conditions that were appalling. For example, he discovered an apartment of one room in which three men, two women, and several children--the members of two families and a male boarder--ate, slept, lived, and made cigars. "The tobacco was stowed about everywhere, alongside the foul bedding, and in a corner where there were scraps of food." These conditions were not exceptional; they were only a little worse than was usual.

Roosevelt did not oppose the bill; he fought for it and it passed. Then he appeared before Governor Cleveland to argue for it on behalf of the Cigar-Makers' Union. The Governor hesitated, but finally signed it. The Court of Appeals declared it unconstitutional, in a smug and well-fed decision, which spoke unctuously of the "hallowed" influences of the "home." It was a wicked decision, because it was purely academic, and was removed as far as the fixed stars from the actual facts of life. But it had one good result. It began the making of Theodore Roosevelt into a champion of social justice, for, as he himself said, it was this case which first waked him "to a dim and partial understanding of the fact that the courts were not necessarily the best judges of what should be done to better social and industrial conditions."

When, a quarter, of a century later, Roosevelt left the Presidency and became Contributing Editor of The Outlook, almost his first contribution to that journal was entitled "A Judicial Experience." It told the story of this law and its annulment by the court. Mr. William Travers Jerome wrote a letter to The Outlook, taking Roosevelt sharply to task for his criticism of the court. It fell to the happy lot of the writer as a cub editor to reply editorially to Mr. Jerome. I did so with gusto and with particularity. As Mr. Roosevelt left the office on his way to the steamer that was to take him to Africa to hunt non-political big game, he said to me, who had seen him only once before: "That was bully. You have done just what my Cabinet members used to do for me in Washington. When a question rose that demanded action, I used to act. Then I would tell Root or Taft to find out and tell me why what I had done was legal and justified. Well done, coworker." Is it any wonder that Theodore Roosevelt had made in that moment another ardent supporter?

Those first years in the political arena were not only a fighting time, they were a formative time. The young Roosevelt had to discover a philosophy of political action which would satisfy him. He speedily found one that suited his temperament and his keen sense of reality. He found no reason to depart from it to the day of his death. Long afterward he told his good friend Jacob Riis how he arrived at it. This was the way of it:

"I suppose that my head was swelled. It would not be strange if it was. I stood out for my own opinion, alone. I took the best mugwump stand: my own conscience, my own judgment, were to decide in all things. I would listen to no argument, no advice. I took the isolated peak on every issue, and my people left me. When I looked around, before the session was well under way, I found myself alone. I was absolutely deserted. The people didn't understand. The men from Erie, from Suffolk, from anywhere, would not work with me. 'He won't listen to anybody,' they said, and I would not. My isolated peak had become a valley; every bit of influence I had was gone. The things I wanted to do I was powerless to accomplish. What did I do? I looked the ground over and made up my mind that there were several other excellent people there, with honest opinions of the right, even though they differed from me. I turned in to help them, and they turned to and gave me a hand. And so we were able to get things done. We did not agree in all things, but we did in some, and those we pulled at together. That was my first lesson in real politics. It is just this: if you are cast on a desert island with only a screw-driver, a hatchet, and a chisel to make a boat with, why, go make the best one you can. It would be better if you had a saw, but you haven't. So with men. Here is my friend in Congress who is a good man, a strong man, but cannot be made to believe in some things which I trust. It is too bad that he doesn't look at it as I do, but he DOES NOT, and we have to work together as we can. There is a point, of course, where a man must take the isolated peak and break with it all for clear principle, but until it comes he must work, if he would be of use, with men as they are. As long as the good in them overbalances the evil, let him work with that for the best that can be got."

From the moment that he had learned this valuable lesson--and Roosevelt never needed to learn a lesson twice--he had his course in public life marked out before him. He believed ardently in getting things done. He was no theoretical reformer. He would never take the wrong road; but, if he could not go as far as he wanted to along the right road, he would go as far as he could, and bide his time for the rest.

He would not compromise a hair's breadth on a principle; he would compromise cheerfully on a method which did not mean surrender of the principle. He perceived that there were in political life many bad men who were thoroughly efficient and many good men who would have liked to accomplish high results but who were thoroughly inefficient. He realized that if he wished to accomplish anything for the country his business was to combine decency and efficiency; to be a thoroughly practical man of high ideals who did his best to reduce those ideals to actual practice. This was the choice that he made in those first days, the companionable road of practical idealism rather than the isolated peak of idealistic ineffectiveness.

A hard test of his political philosophy came in 1884 just after he had left the Legislature. He was selected as one of the four delegates at large from New York to the Republican National Convention. There he advocated vigorously the nomination of Senator George F. Edmunds for the Presidency. But the more popular candidate with the delegates was James G. Blaine. Roosevelt did not believe in Blaine, who was a politician of the professional type and who had a reputation that was not immaculate. The better element among the delegates fought hard against Blaine's nomination, with Roosevelt wherever the blows were shrewdest. But their efforts were of no avail. Too many party hacks had come to the Convention, determined to nominate Blaine, and they put the slate through with a whoop.

Then, every Republican in active politics who was anything but a rubber stamp politician had a difficult problem to face. Should he support Blaine, in whom he could have no confidence and for whom he could have no respect, or should he "bolt"? A large group decided to bolt. They organized the Mugwump party--the epithet was flung at them with no friendly intent by Charles A. Dana of the New York Sun, but they made of it an honorable title--under the leadership of George William Curtis and Carl Schurz. Their announced purpose was to defeat the Republicans, from whose ranks they had seceded, and in this attempt they were successful.

Roosevelt, however, made the opposite decision. Indeed, he had made the decision before he entered the Convention. It was characteristic of him not to wait until the choice was upon him but to look ahead and make up his mind just which course he would take if and when a certain contingency arose. I remember that once in the later days at Oyster Bay he said to me, "They say I am impulsive. It isn't true. The fact is that on all the important things that may come up for decision in my life, I have thought the thing out in advance and know what I will do. So when the moment comes, I don't have to stop to work it out then. My decision is already made. I have only to put it into action. It looks like impulsiveness. It is nothing of the sort."

So, in 1884, when Roosevelt met his first problem in national politics, he already knew what he would do. He would support Blaine, for he was a party man. The decision wounded many of his friends. But it was the natural result of his political philosophy. He believed in political parties as instruments for securing the translation into action of the popular will. He perceived that the party system, as distinguished from the group system of the continental peoples, was the Anglo-Saxon, the American way of doing things. He wanted to get things done. There was only one thing that he valued more than achievement and that was the right. Therefore, until it became a clean issue between right and wrong, he would stick to the instrument which seemed to him the most efficient for getting things done. So he stuck to his party, in spite of his distaste for its candidate, and saw it go down in defeat.

Roosevelt never changed his mind about this important matter. He was a party man to the end. In 1912 he left his old party on what he believed to be--and what was--a naked moral issue. But he did not become an independent. He created a new party.

# CHAPTER III. THE CHAMPION OF CIVIL SERVICE REFORM

The four years after the Cleveland-Blaine campaign were divided into two parts for Roosevelt by another political experience, which also resulted in defeat. He was nominated by the Republicans and a group of independents for Mayor of New York. His two opponents were Abram S. Hewitt, a business man of standing who had been inveigled, no one knows how, into lending respectability to the Tammany ticket in a critical moment, and Henry George, the father of the Single Tax doctrine, who had been nominated by a conference of some one hundred and seventy-five labor organizations. Roosevelt fought his best on a personal platform of "no class or caste" but "honest and economical government on behalf of the general wellbeing." But the inevitable happened. Tammany slipped in between its divided enemies and made off with the victory.

The rest of the four years he spent partly in ranch life out in the Dakotas, partly in writing history and biography at home and in travel. The life on the ranch and in the hunting camps finished the business, so resolutely begun in the outdoor gymnasium on Twentieth Street, of developing a physical equipment adequate for any call he could make upon it. This sojourn on the plains gave him, too, an intimate knowledge of the frontier type of American. Theodore Roosevelt loved his fellow men. What is more, he was always interested in them, not abstractly and in the mass, but concretely and in the individual. He believed in them. He knew their strength and their virtues, and he rejoiced in them. He realized their weaknesses and their softnesses and fought them hard. It was all this that made him the thoroughgoing democrat that he was. "The average American," I have heard him say a hundred times to all kinds of audiences, "is a pretty good fellow, and his wife is a still better fellow." He not only enjoyed those years in the West to the full, but he profited by them as well. They broadened and deepened his knowledge of what the American people were and meant. They made vivid to him the value of the simple, robust virtues of self-reliance, courage, self-denial, tolerance, and justice. The influence of those hard-riding years was with him as a great asset to the end of his life.

In the Presidential campaign of 1888, Roosevelt was on the firing line again, fighting for the Republican candidate, Benjamin Harrison. When Mr. Harrison was elected, he would have liked to put the young campaigner into the State Department. But Mr. Blaine, who became Secretary of State, did not care to have his plain-spoken opponent and critic under him. So the President offered Roosevelt the post of Civil Service Commissioner.

The spoils system had become habitual and traditional in American public life by sixty years of practice. It had received its first high sanction in the cynical words of a New York politician, "To the victor belong the spoils." Politicians looked upon it as a normal accompaniment of their activities. The public looked upon it with indifference. But finally a group of irrepressible reformers succeeded in getting the camel's nose under the flap of the tent. A law was passed establishing a Commission which was to introduce the merit system. But even then neither the politicians nor the public, nor the Commission itself, took the matter very seriously. The Commission was in the habit of carrying on its functions perfunctorily and unobtrusively. But nothing could be perfunctory where Roosevelt was. He would never permit things to be done--or left undone unobtrusively, when what was needed was to obtrude the matter forcibly on the public mind. He was a profound believer in the value of publicity.

When Roosevelt became Commissioner things began swiftly to happen. He had two firm convictions: that laws were made to be enforced, in the letter and in the spirit; and that the only thing worth while in the world was to get things done. He believed with a hot conviction in decency, honesty, and efficiency in public as in private life.

For six years he fought and infused his fellow Commissioners with some of his fighting spirit. They were good men but easy-going until the right leadership came along. The first effort of the Commission under the new leadership was to secure the genuine enforcement of the law. The backbone of the merit system was the competitive examination. This was not because such examinations are the infallible way to get good public servants, but because they are the best way that has yet been devised to keep out bad public servants, selected for private reasons having nothing to do with the public welfare. The effort to make these examinations and the subsequent appointments of real service to the nation rather than to the politicians naturally brought the Commission into conflict with many men of low ideals, both in Congress and without. Roosevelt found a number of men in Congress--like Senator Lodge, Senator Davis of Minnesota, Senator Platt of Connecticut, and Congressman (afterward President) McKinley--who were sincerely and vigorously opposed to the spoils system. But there were numbers of other Senators and Congressmen who hated the whole reform--everything connected with it and everybody who championed it. "Sometimes," Roosevelt said of these men, "to use a legal phrase, their hatred was for cause, and sometimes it was peremptory--that is, sometimes the Commission interfered with their most efficient, and incidentally most corrupt and unscrupulous supporters, and at other times, where there was no such interference, a man nevertheless had an innate dislike of anything that tended to decency in government."

Conflict with these men was inevitable. Sometimes their opposition took the form of trying to cut down the appropriation for the Commission.

Then the Commission, on Roosevelt's suggestion, would try the effect of holding no examinations in the districts of the Senators or Congressmen who had voted against the appropriation. The response from the districts was instantaneous. Frantic appeals came to the Commission from aspirants for office. The reply would be suave and courteous. One can imagine Roosevelt dictating it with a glint in his eye and a snap of the jaw, and when it was typed, inserting a sting in the tail in the form of an interpolated sentence in his own vigorous and rugged script. Those added sentences, without which any typewritten Roosevelt letter might almost be declared to be a forgery, so uniformly did the impulse to add them seize him, were always the most interesting feature of a communication from him. The letter would inform the protesting one that unfortunately the appropriation had been cut, so that examinations could not be held in every district, and that obviously the Commission could not neglect the districts of those Congressmen who believed in the reform and therefore in the examinations. The logical next step for the hungry aspirant was to transfer the attack to his Congressman or Senator. In the long run, by this simple device of backfiring, which may well have been a reminiscence of prairie fire days in the West, the Commission obtained enough money to carry on.

There were other forms of attack tried by the spoils-loving legislators. One was investigation by a congressional committee. But the appearance of Roosevelt before such an investigating body invariably resulted in a "bully time" for him and a peculiarly disconcerting time for his opponents.

One of the Republican floor leaders in the House in those days was Congressman Grosvenor from Ohio. In an unwary moment Mr. Grosvenor attacked the Commission on the floor of the House in picturesque fashion. Roosevelt promptly asked that Mr. Grosvenor be invited to meet him before a congressional committee which was at that moment investigating the activities of the Commission. The Congressman did not accept the invitation until he heard that Roosevelt was leaving Washington for his ranch in the West. Then he notified the committee that he would be glad to meet Commissioner Roosevelt at one of its sessions. Roosevelt immediately postponed his journey and met him. Mr. Grosvenor, says Roosevelt in his Autobiography, "proved to be a person of happily treacherous memory, so that the simple expedient of arranging his statements in pairs was sufficient to reduce him to confusion." He declared to the committee, for instance, that he did not want to repeal the Civil Service Law and had never said so. Roosevelt produced one of Mr. Grosvenor's speeches in which he had said, "I will not only vote to strike out this provision, but I will vote to repeal the whole law." Grosvenor declared that there was no inconsistency between these two statements. At another point in his testimony, he asserted that a certain applicant for office, who had, as he put it, been fraudulently credited to his congressional district, had never lived in that district or in Ohio, so far as he knew. Roosevelt brought forth a letter in which the Congressman himself had categorically stated that the man in question was not only a legal resident of his district but was actually living there then. He explained, says Roosevelt, "first, that he had not written the letter; second, that he had forgotten he had written the letter; and, third, that he was grossly deceived when he wrote it." Grosvenor at length accused Roosevelt of a lack of humor in not appreciating that his statements were made "in a jesting way," and declared that "a Congressman making a speech on the floor of the House of Representatives was perhaps in a little different position from a witness on the witness stand." Finally he rose with dignity and, asserting his constitutional right not to be questioned elsewhere as to what he said on the floor of the House, withdrew, leaving Roosevelt and the Committee equally delighted with the opera bouffe in which he had played the leading part.

In the Roosevelt days the Commission carried on its work, as of course it should, without thought of party. It can be imagined how it made the "good" Republicans rage when one of the results of the impartial application system was to put into office from the Southern States a hundred or two Democrats. The critics of the Commission were equally non-partisan; there was no politics in spoilsmanship. The case of Mr. Grosvenor was matched by that of Senator Gorman of Maryland, the Democratic leader in the Senate. Mr. Gorman told upon the floor of the Senate the affecting story of "a bright young man from Baltimore," a Sunday School scholar, well recommended by his pastor, who aspired to be a letter carrier. He appeared before the Commission for examination, and, according to Mr. Gorman, he was first asked to describe the shortest route from Baltimore to China. The "bright young man" replied brightly, according to Mr. Gorman, that he didn't want to go from Baltimore to China, and therefore had never concerned himself about the choice of routes. He was then asked, according to Mr. Gorman, all about the steamship lines from America to Europe; then came questions in geology, and finally in chemistry. The Commission thereupon turned the bright young applicant down. The Senator's speech was masterly. It must have made the spoilsmen chuckle and the friends of civil service reform squirm. It had neither of these effects on Roosevelt. It merely exploded him into action like a finger on a hair-trigger. First of all, he set about hunting down the facts. Facts were his favorite ammunition in a fight. They have such a powerful punch. A careful investigation of all the examination papers which the Commission had set revealed not a single question like those from which the "bright young man," according to Mr. Gorman, had suffered. So Roosevelt wrote to the Senator asking for the name of the "bright young man." There was no response. He also asked, in case Mr. Gorman did not care to reveal his identity, the date of the examination. Still no reply. Roosevelt offered to give to any representative whom Mr. Gorman would send to the Commission's offices all the aid he could in discovering in the files any such questions. The offer was ignored. But the Senator expressed himself as so shocked at this doubting of the word of his brilliant protege that he was unable to answer the letter at all.

Roosevelt thereupon announced publicly that no such questions had ever been asked. Mr. Gorman was gravely injured by the whole incident. Later he declared in the Senate that he had received a "very impudent letter" from the young Commissioner, and that he had been "cruelly" called to account because he had tried to right a "great wrong" which the Commission had committed. Roosevelt's retort was to tell the whole story publicly, closing with this delightful passage:

"High-minded, sensitive Mr. Gorman. Clinging, trustful Mr. Gorman. Nothing could shake his belief in the "bright young man." Apparently he did not even try to find out his name--if he had a name; in fact, his name like everything else about him, remains to this day wrapped in the Stygian mantle of an abysmal mystery. Still less has Mr. Gorman tried to verify the statements made to him. It is enough for him that they were made. No harsh suspicion, no stern demand for evidence or proof, appeals to his artless and unspoiled soul. He believes whatever he is told, even when he has forgotten the name of the teller, or never knew it. It would indeed be difficult to find an instance of a more abiding confidence in human nature--even in anonymous human nature. And this is the end of the tale of the Arcadian Mr. Gorman and his elusive friend, the bright young man without a name."

Even so near the beginning of his career, Roosevelt showed himself perfectly fearless in attack. He would as soon enter the lists against a Senator as a Congressman, as soon challenge a Cabinet member as either. He did not even hesitate to make it uncomfortable for the President to whom he owed his continuance in office. His only concern was for the honor of the public service which he was in office to defend.

One day he appeared at a meeting of the Executive Committee of the Civil Service Reform Association. George William Curtis was presiding, and Roosevelt's old friend, George Haven Putnam, who tells the story, was also present. Roosevelt began by hurling a solemn but hearty imprecation at the head of the Postmaster General. He went on to explain that his explosive wrath was due to the fact that that particular gentleman was the most pernicious of all the enemies of the merit system. It was one of the functions of the Civil Service Commission, as Roosevelt saw it, to put a stop to improper political activities by Federal employees. Such activities were among the things that the Civil Service law was intended to prevent. They strengthened the hands of the political machines and the bosses, and at the same time weakened the efficiency of the service. Roosevelt had from time to time reported to the Postmaster General what some of the Post Office employees were doing in political ways to the detriment of the service. His account of what happened was this:

"I placed before the Postmaster-General sworn statements in regard to these political activities and the only reply I could secure was, 'This is all second-hand evidence.' Then I went up to Baltimore at the invitation of our good friend, a member of the National Committee, Charles J. Bonaparte. Bonaparte said that he could bring me into direct touch with some of the matters complained about. He took me to the primary meetings with some associate who knew by name the carriers and the customs officials. I was able to see going on the work of political assessments, and I heard the instructions given to the carriers and others in regard to the moneys that they were to collect. I got the names of some of these men recorded in my memorandum book. I then went back to Washington, swore myself in as a witness before myself as Commissioner, and sent the sworn statement to the Postmaster-General with the word, 'This at least is firsthand evidence.' I still got no reply, and after waiting a few days, I put the whole material before the President with a report. This report has been pigeonholed by the President, and I have now come to New York to see what can be done to get the evidence before the public. You will understand that the head of a department, having made a report to the President, can do nothing further with the material until the President permits."

Roosevelt went back to Washington with the sage advice to ask the Civil Service Committee of the House to call upon him to give evidence in regard to the working of the Civil Service Act. He could then get into the record his first-hand evidence as well as a general statement of the bad practices which were going on. This evidence, when printed as a report of the congressional committee, could be circulated by the Association. Roosevelt bettered the advice by asking to have the Postmaster General called before the committee at the same time as himself. This was done, but that timid politician replied to the Chairman of the committee that "he would hold himself at the service of the Committee for any date on which Mr. Roosevelt was not to be present." The politicians with uneasy consciences were getting a little wary about face-to-face encounters with the young fighter. Nevertheless Roosevelt's testimony was given and circulated broadcast, as Major Putnam writes, "much to the dissatisfaction of the Postmaster General and probably of the President."

The six years which Roosevelt spent on the Civil Service Commission were for him years of splendid training in the methods and practices of political life. What he learned then stood him in good stead when he came to the Presidency. Those years of Roosevelt's gave an impetus to the cause of civil reform which far surpassed anything it had received until his time. Indeed, it is probably not unfair to say that it has received no greater impulse since.

# CHAPTER IV. HAROUN AL ROOSEVELT

In 1895, at the age of thirty-six, Roosevelt was asked by Mayor Strong of New York City, who had just been elected on an anti-Tammany ticket, to become a member of his Administration. Mayor Strong wanted him for Street Cleaning Commissioner. Roosevelt definitely refused that office, on the ground that he had no special fitness for it, but accepted readily the Mayor's subsequent proposal that he should become President of the Police Commission, knowing that there was a job that he could do.

There was plenty of work to be done in the Police Department. The conditions under which it must be done were dishearteningly unfavorable. In the first place, the whole scheme of things was wrong. The Police Department was governed by one of those bi-partisan commissions which well-meaning theorists are wont sometimes to set up when they think that the important thing in government is to have things arranged so that nobody can do anything harmful. The result often is that nobody can do anything at all. There were four Commissioners, two supposed to belong to one party and two to the other. There was also a Chief of Police, appointed by the Commission, who could not be removed without a trial subject to review by the courts. The scheme put a premium on intriguing and obstruction. It was far inferior to the present plan of a single Commissioner with full power, subject only to the Mayor who appoints him.

But there is an interesting lesson to be learned from a comparison between the New York Police Department as it is today and as it was twenty-five years ago. Then the scheme of organization was thoroughly bad--and the department was at its high-water mark of honest and effective activity. Now the scheme of organization is excellent--but the less said about the way it works the better. The answer to the riddle is this: today the New York police force is headed by Tammany; the name of the particular Tammany man who is Commissioner does not matter. In those days the head was Roosevelt.

There were many good men on the force then as now. What Roosevelt said of the men of his time is as true today: "There are no better men anywhere than the men of the New York police force; and when they go bad it is because the system is wrong, and because they are not given the chance to do the good work they can do and would rather do." The first fight that Roosevelt found on his hands was to keep politics and every kind of favoritism absolutely out of the force. During his six years as Civil Service Commissioner he had learned much about the way to get good men into the public service. He was now able to put his own theories into practice. His method was utterly simple and incontestably right. "As far as was humanly possible, the appointments and promotions were made without regard to any question except the fitness of the man and the needs of the service." That was all. "We paid," he said, "not the slightest attention to a man's politics or creed, or where he was born, so long as he was an American citizen." But it was not easy to convince either the politicians or the public that the Commission really meant what it said. In view of the long record of unblushing corruption in connection with every activity in the Police Department, and of the existence, which was a matter of common knowledge, of a regular tariff for appointments and promotions, it is little wonder that the news that every one on, or desiring to get on, the force would have a square deal was received with scepticism. But such was the fact. Roosevelt brought the whole situation out into the open, gave the widest possible publicity to what the Commission was doing, and went hotly after any intimation of corruption.

One secret of his success here as everywhere else was that he did things himself. He knew things of his own knowledge. One evening he went down to the Bowery to speak at a branch of the Young Men's Christian Association. There he met a young Jew, named Raphael, who had recently displayed unusual courage and physical prowess in rescuing women and children from a burning building. Roosevelt suggested that he try the examination for entrance to the force. Young Raphael did so, was successful, and became a policeman of the best type. He and his family, said Roosevelt, "have been close friends of mine ever since." Another comment which he added is delicious and illuminating: "To show our community of feeling and our grasp of the facts of life, I may mention that we were almost the only men in the

Police Department who picked Fitzsimmons as a winner against Corbett." There is doubtless much in this little incident shocking to the susceptibilities of many who would consider themselves among the "best" people. But Roosevelt would care little for that. He was a real democrat; and to his great soul there was nothing either incongruous or undesirable in having--and in admitting that he had--close friends in an East Side Jewish family just over from Russia. He believed, too, in "the strenuous life," in boxing and in prize fighting when it was clean. He could meet a subordinate as man to man on the basis of such a personal matter as their respective judgment of two prize fighters, without relaxing in the slightest degree their official relations. He was a man of realities, who knew how to preserve the real distinctions of life without insisting on the artificial ones.

One of the best allies that Roosevelt had was Jacob A. Riis, that extraordinary man with the heart of a child, the courage of a lion, and the spirit of a crusader, who came from Denmark as an immigrant, tramped the streets of New York and the country roads without a place to lay his head, became one of the best police reporters New York ever knew, and grew to be a flaming force for righteousness in the city of his adoption. His book, "How the Other Half Lives", did more to clean up the worst slums of the city than any other single thing. When the book appeared, Roosevelt went to Mr. Riis's office, found him out, and left a card which said simply, "I have read your book. I have come down to help." When Roosevelt became Police Commissioner, Riis was in the Tribune Police Bureau in Mulberry Street, opposite Police Headquarters, already a well valued friend. Roosevelt took him for guide, and together they tramped about the dark spots of the city in the night hours when the underworld slips its mask and bares its arm to strike. Roosevelt had to know for himself. He considered that he had two duties as Police Commissioner: one to make the police force an honest and effective public servant; the other to use his position "to help in making the city a better place in which to live and work for those to whom the conditions of life and labor were hardest." These night wanderings of "Haroun al Roosevelt," as some one successfully ticketed him in allusion to the great Caliph's similar expeditions, were powerful aids to the tightening up of discipline and to the encouragement of good work by patrolmen and roundsmen. The unfaithful or the easy-going man on the beat, who allowed himself to be beguiled by the warmth and cheer of a saloon back-room, or to wander away from his duty for his own purposes, was likely to be confronted by the black slouch hat and the gleaming spectacles of a tough-set figure that he knew as the embodiment of relentless justice. But the faithful knew no less surely that he was their best friend and champion.

In the old days of "the system," not only appointment to the force and promotion, but recognition of exceptional achievement went by favor. The policeman who risked his life in the pursuit of duty and accomplished some big thing against great odds could not be sure of the reward to which he was entitled unless he had political pull. It was even the rule in the Department that the officer who spoiled his uniform in rescuing man, woman, or child from the waters of the river must get a new one at his own expense. "The system" knew neither justice nor fair play. It knew nothing but the cynical phrase of Richard Croker, Tammany Hall's famous boss, "my own pocket all the time." But Roosevelt changed all that. He had not been in Mulberry Street a month before that despicable rule about the uniform was blotted out. His whole term of office on the Police Board was marked by acts of recognition of bravery and faithful service. Many times he had to dig the facts out for himself or ran upon them by accident. There was no practice in the Department of recording the good work done by the men on the force so that whoever would might read.

Roosevelt enjoyed this part of his task heartily. He believed vigorously in courage, hardihood, and daring. What is more, he believed with his whole soul in men. It filled him with pure joy when he discovered a man of the true stalwart breed who held his own life as nothing when his duty was at stake.

During his two years' service, he and his fellow Commissioners singled out more than a hundred men for special mention because of some feat of heroism. Two cases which he describes in his "Autobiography" are typical of the rest. One was that of an old fellow, a veteran of the Civil War, who was a roundsman. Roosevelt noticed one day that he had saved a woman from drowning and called him before him to investigate the matter. The veteran officer was not a little nervous and agitated as he produced his record. He had grown gray in the service and had performed feat after feat of heroism; but his complete lack of political backing had kept him from further promotion. In twenty-two years on the force he had saved some twenty-five persons from drowning, to say nothing of rescuing several from burning buildings. Twice Congress had passed special acts to permit the Secretary of the Treasury to give him a medal for distinguished gallantry in saving life. He had received other medals from the Life Saving Society and from the Police Department itself. The one thing that he could not achieve was adequate promotion, although his record was spotless. When Roosevelt's attention was attracted to him, he received his promotion then and there. "It may be worth mentioning," says Roosevelt, "that he kept on saving life after he was given his sergeantcy."

The other case was that of a patrolman who seemed to have fallen into the habit of catching burglars. Roosevelt noticed that he caught two in successive weeks, the second time under unusual conditions. The policeman saw the burglar emerging from a house soon after midnight and gave chase. The fugitive ran toward Park Avenue. The New York Central Railroad runs under that avenue, and there is a succession of openings in the top of the tunnel. The burglar took a desperate chance by dropping through one of the openings, at the imminent risk of breaking his neck. "Now the burglar," says Roosevelt, "was running for his liberty, and it was the part of wisdom for him to imperil life and limb; but the policeman was merely doing his duty, and nobody could have blamed him for not taking the jump. However, he jumped; and in this particular case the hand of the Lord was heavy upon the unrighteous. The burglar had the breath knocked out of him, and the 'cop' didn't. When his victim could walk, the officer trotted him around to the station house." When Roosevelt had discovered that the patrolman's record showed him to be sober, trustworthy, and strictly attentive to duty, he secured his promotion at once.

So the Police Commission, during those two years, under the driving force of Roosevelt's example and spirit, went about the regeneration of the force whose former proud title of "The Finest" had been besmirched by those who should have been its champions and defenders. Politics, favoritism, and corruption were knocked out of the department with all the thoroughness that the absurd bipartisan scheme of administration would permit.

The most spectacular fight of all was against the illegal operations of the saloons. The excise law forbade the sale of liquor on Sunday. But the police, under orders from "higher up," enforced the law with discretion. The saloons which paid blackmail, or which enjoyed the protection of some powerful Tammany chieftain, sold liquor on Sunday with impunity. Only those whose owners were recalcitrant or without influence were compelled to obey the law.

Now a goodly proportion of the population of New York, as of any great city, objects strenuously to having its personal habits interfered with by the community. This is just as true now in the days of prohibition as it was then in the days of "Sunday closing." So when Roosevelt came into office with the simple, straightforward conviction that laws on the statute books were intended to be enforced and proceeded to close all the saloons on Sunday, the result was inevitable. The professional politicians foamed at the mouth. The yellow press shrieked and lied. The saloon-keepers and the sharers of their illicit profits wriggled and squirmed. But the saloons were closed. The law was enforced without fear or favor. The Sunday sale of liquor disappeared from the city, until a complaisant judge, ruling upon the provision of the law which permitted drink to be sold with a meal, decreed that one pretzel, even when accompanied by seventeen beers, made a "meal." No amount of honesty and fearlessness in the enforcement of the law could prevail against such judicial aid and comfort to the cause of nullification. The main purpose of Roosevelt's fight for Sunday closing, the stopping of blackmail, was, however, achieved. A standard of law enforcement was set which shows what can be done even with an unpopular law, and in New York City itself, if the will to deal honestly and without cowardice is there.

So the young man who was "ever a fighter" went on his way, fighting evil to the death wherever he found it, achieving results, making friends eagerly and enemies blithely, learning, broadening, growing. Already he had made a distinct impression upon his times.

# CHAPTER V. FIGHTING AND BREAKFASTING WITH PLATT

From the New York Police Department Roosevelt was called by President McKinley to Washington in 1897, to become Assistant Secretary of the Navy. After a year there--the story of which belongs elsewhere in this volume--he resigned to go to Cuba as Lieutenant-Colonel of the Rough Riders. He was just as prominent in that war for liberty and justice as the dimensions of the conflict permitted. He was accustomed in after years to say with deprecating humor, when talking to veterans of the Civil War, "It wasn't much of a war, but it was all the war we had." It made him Governor of New York.

When he landed with his regiment at Montauk Point from Cuba, he was met by two delegations. One consisted of friends from his own State who were political independents; the other came from the head of the Republican political machine.

Both wanted him as a candidate for Governor. The independents were anxious to have him make a campaign against the Old Guard of both the standard parties, fighting Richard Croker, the cynical Tammany boss, on the one side, and Thomas C. Platt, the "easy boss" of the Republicans, on the other. Tom Platt did not want him at all. But he did want to win the election, and he knew that he must have something superlatively fine to offer, if he was to have any hope of carrying the discredited Republican party to victory. So he swallowed whatever antipathy he may have had and offered the nomination to Roosevelt. This was before the days when the direct primary gave the plain voters an opportunity to upset the calculations of a political boss.

Senator Platt's emissary, Lemuel Ely Quigg, in a two hours' conversation in the tent at Montauk, asked some straight-from-the-shoulder questions. The answers he received were just as unequivocal. Mr. Quigg wanted a plain statement as to whether or not Roosevelt wanted the nomination. He wanted to know what Roosevelt's attitude would be toward the organization in the event of his election, whether or not he would "make war" on Mr. Platt and his friends, or whether he would confer with them and give fair consideration to their point of view as to party policy and public interest. In short, he wanted a frank definition of Roosevelt's attitude towards existing party conditions. He got precisely that. Here it is, in Roosevelt's own words:

"I replied that I should like to be nominated, and if nominated would promise to throw myself into the campaign with all possible energy. I said that I should not make war on Mr. Platt or anybody else if war could be avoided; that what I wanted was to be Governor and not a faction leader; that I certainly would confer with the organization men, as with everybody else who seemed to me to have knowledge of and interest in public affairs, and that as to Mr. Platt and the organization leaders, I would do so in the sincere hope that there might always result harmony of opinion and purpose; but that while I would try to get on well with the organization, the organization must with equal sincerity strive to do what I regarded as essential for the public good; and that in every case, after full consideration of what everybody had to say who might possess real knowledge of the matter, I should have to act finally as my own judgment and conscience dictated and administer the State government as I thought it ought to be administered.... I told him to tell the Senator that while I would talk freely with him, and had no intention of becoming a factional leader with a personal organization, yet I must have direct personal relations with everybody, and get their views at first hand whenever I so desired, because I could not have one man speaking for all."[1]

This was straight Roosevelt talk. It was probably the first time that the "easy boss" had received such a response to his overtures. History does not record how he liked it; but at least he accepted it. Subsequent events suggest that he was either unwilling to believe or incapable of understanding that the Colonel of the Rough Riders meant precisely what he said. But Platt found out his mistake. He was not the first or the last politician to have that experience.

So Roosevelt was nominated, made a gruelling campaign, was elected by a small but sufficient majority, in a year when any other Republican candidate would

---

1  Autobiography

probably have been "snowed under," and became Governor seventeen years after he entered public life. He was now forty years old.

The governorship of Theodore Roosevelt was marked by a deal of fine constructive legislation and administration. But it was even more notable for the new standard which it set for the relationship in which the executive of a great State should stand to his office, to the public welfare, to private interests, and to the leaders of his party. Before Roosevelt's election there was need for a revision of the standard. In those days it was accepted as a matter of course, at least in practice, that the party boss was the overlord of the constitutional representatives of the people. Appointments were made primarily for the good of the party and only incidentally in the public interest. The welfare of the party was closely bound up with the profit of special interests, such as public service corporations and insurance companies. The prevalent condition of affairs was shrewdly summed up in a satiric paraphrase of Lincoln's conception of the American ideal: "Government of the people, by the bosses, for the special interests." The interests naturally repaid this zealous care for their well-being by contributions to the party funds.

Platt was one of the most nearly absolute party bosses that the American system of machine politics has produced. In spite of the fair warning which he had already received, both directly from Roosevelt's own words, and indirectly from his whole previous career, he was apparently surprised and unquestionably annoyed when he found that he was not to be the new Governor's master. The trouble began before Roosevelt took office. At a conference one day Platt asked Roosevelt if there were any members of the Assembly whom he would like to have assigned to special committees. Roosevelt was surprised at the question, as he had not known that the Speaker of the Assembly, who appoints the committees, had yet been agreed upon by the Assemblymen-elect. He expressed his surprise. But Mr. Platt enlightened him, saying, "Of course, whoever we choose as Speaker will agree beforehand to make the appointments we wish." Roosevelt has recorded the mental note which he thereupon made, that if they tried the same process with the Governor-elect they would find themselves mistaken. In a few days they did try it--and discovered their mistake.

Platt asked Roosevelt to come to see him. The Senator being an old and physically feeble man, Roosevelt went. Platt handed him a telegram from a certain man, accepting with pleasure his appointment as Superintendent of Public Works. This was one of the most important appointive offices in the State Administration. It was especially so at this time in view of the scandals which had arisen under the previous Administration over the Erie Canal, the most important responsibility of this department. Now, the man whom the boss had picked out was an excellent fellow, whom Roosevelt liked and whom, incidentally, he later appointed to an office which he filled in admirable fashion. But Roosevelt had no intention of having any one but himself select the members of his Administration. He said so frankly and simply. The Senator raged. He was unaccustomed to such independence of spirit. Roosevelt was courteous but firm. The irresistible force had met the immovable obstacle--and the force capitulated. The telegraphic acceptance was not accepted. The appointment was not made.

Mr. Platt was a wise man, even if he was arrogant. He knew when he had met one whom he could not drive. So he did not break with the new Governor. Roosevelt was wise, too, although he was honest. So he did not break with the "easy boss." His failure to do so was a disappointment to his impractical friends and supporters, who were more concerned with theoretical goodness than with achievement.

Roosevelt worked with Platt and the party machine whenever he could. He fought only when he must. When he fought, he won. In Senator Platt's "Autobiography", the old boss paid this tribute to the young fighter whom he had made Governor: "Roosevelt had from the first agreed that he would consult me on all questions of appointments, Legislature or party policy. He religiously fulfilled this pledge, although he frequently did just what he pleased."

One of the things that particularly grieved the theoretical idealists and the chronic objectors was the fact that Roosevelt used on occasion to take breakfast with Senator Platt. They did not seem to think it possible that a Governor could accept the hospitality of a boss without taking orders from him. But Mr. Platt knew better, if they did not. He was never under any illusions as to the extent of his influence with Roosevelt. It vanished precisely at the point where the selfish interests of the party and the wishes of the boss collided with the public welfare. The facts about the famous breakfasts are plain enough. The Governor was in Albany, the Senator in Washington. Both found it easy to get to New York on Saturday. It was natural that they should from time to time have matters to discuss for both were leaders in their party. Mr. Platt was a feeble man, who found it difficult to get about. Roosevelt was a chivalrous man, who believed that courtesy and consideration were due to age and weakness. In addition, he liked to make every minute count. So he used to go, frankly and openly, to the Senator's hotel for breakfast. He was not one of that class which he has described as composed of "solemn reformers of the tom-fool variety, who, according to their custom, paid attention to the name and not the thing." He cared only for the reality; the appearance mattered little to him.

The tom-fool reformers who criticized Roosevelt for meeting Platt at break-fast were not even good observers. If they had been, they would have realized that when Roosevelt breakfasted with Platt, it generally meant that he was trying to reconcile the Senator to something he was going to do which the worthy boss did not like. For instance, Roosevelt once wrote to Platt, who was trying to get him to promote a certain judge over the head of another judge: "There is a strong feeling among the judges and the leading members of the bar that Judge Y ought not to have Judge X jumped over his head, and I do not see my way clear to doing it. I am inclined to think that the solution I mentioned to you is the solution I shall have to adopt. Remember the breakfast at Douglas Robinson's at 8:30." It is probable that the Governor enjoyed that breakfast more than did the Senator. So it usually was with the famous breakfasts. "A series of breakfasts was always the prelude to some active warfare."

For Roosevelt and Platt still had their pitched battles. The most epic of them all was fought over the reappointment of the State Superintendent of Insurance. The incumbent was Louis F. Payn, a veteran petty boss from a country district and one of Platt's right-hand men. Roosevelt discovered that Payn had been involved in compromising relations with certain financiers in New York with whom he "did not deem it expedient that the Superintendent of Insurance, while such, should have any intimate and money-making relations." The Governor therefore decided not to reappoint him. Platt issued an ultimatum that Payn must be reappointed or he would fight. He pointed out that in case of a fight Payn would stay in anyway, since the consent of the State Senate was necessary not only to appoint a man to office but to remove him from office. The Governor replied cheerfully that he had made up his mind and that Payn would not be retained. If he could not get his successor confirmed, he would make the appointment as soon as the Legislature adjourned, and the appointment would stand at least until the Legislature met again. Platt declared in turn that Payn would be reinstated as soon as the Legislature reconvened. Roosevelt admitted the possibility, but assured his opponent that the process would be repeated as soon as that session came to an end. He added his conviction that, while he might have an uncomfortable time himself, he would guarantee that his opponents would be made more uncomfortable still. Thus the matter stood in the weeks before final action could be taken. Platt was sure that Roosevelt must yield. But once more he did not know his man. It is curious how long it takes feudal overlords to get the measure of a fearless free man.

The political power which the boss wielded was reinforced by pressure from big business interests in New York. Officials of the large insurance companies adopted resolutions asking for Payn's reappointment. But some of them privately and hastily assured the Governor that these resolutions were for public consumption only, and that they would be delighted to have Payn superseded. Roosevelt strove to make it clear again and again that he was not fighting the organization as such, and announced his readiness to appoint any one of several men who were good organization men--only he would not retain Lou Payn nor appoint any man of his type. The matter moved along to the final scene, which took place at the Union League Club in New York.

Mr. Platt's chief lieutenant asked for a meeting with the Governor. The request was granted. The emissary went over the ground thoroughly. He declared that Platt would never yield. He explained that he was certain to win the fight, and that he wished to save Roosevelt from such a lamentable disaster as the end of his political career. Roosevelt again explained at length his position. After half an hour he rose to go. The "subsequent proceedings" he described as follows:

"My visitor repeated that I had this last chance, and that ruin was ahead of me if I refused it; whereas, if I accepted, everything would be made easy. I shook my head and answered, 'There is nothing to add to what I have already said.' He responded, 'You have made up your mind?' and I said, 'I have." He then said, 'You know it means your ruin?' and I answered, 'Well, we will see about that,' and walked toward the door. He said, 'You understand, the fight will begin tomorrow and will be carried on to the bitter end.' I said, 'Yes,' and added, as I reached the door, 'Good night.' Then, as the door opened my opponent, or visitor, whichever one chooses to call him, whose face was as impassive and as inscrutable as that of Mr. John Hamlin in a poker game, said: 'Hold on! We accept. Send in so-and-so (the man I had named). The Senator is very sorry, but he will make no further opposition!' I never saw a bluff carried more resolutely through to the final limit."[2]

One other Homeric fight with the machine was Roosevelt's portion during his Governorship. This time it was not directly with the boss himself but with the boss's liegemen in the Legislature. But the kernel of the whole matter was the same--the selfish interests of big corporations against the public good.

In those days corporations were by common practice privileged creatures. They were accustomed to special treatment from legislatures and administrations. But when Roosevelt was elected Governor, he was determined that no corporation should get a valuable privilege from the State without paying for it. Before long he had become convinced that they ought also to pay for those which they already had, free gifts of the State in those purblind days when corporations were young and coddled. He proposed that public service corporations doing business on franchises granted by the State and by municipalities should be taxed upon the value of the privileges they enjoyed. The corporations naturally enough did not like the proposal. But it was made in no spirit or tone of antagonism to business or of demagogic outcry against those who were prosperous. All that the Governor demanded was a square deal. In his message to the Legislature, he wrote as follows:

"There is evident injustice in the light taxation of corporations. I have not the slightest sympathy with the outcry against corporations as such, or against prosperous men of business. Most of the great material works by which the entire country benefits have been due to the action of individual men, or of aggregates of men, who made money for themselves by doing that which was in the interest of the people as a whole. From an armor plant to a street railway, no work which is really beneficial to the public can be performed to the best advantage of the public save by men of such business capacity that they will not do the work unless they themselves receive ample reward for doing it. The effort to deprive them of an ample reward merely means that they will turn their energies in some other direction; and the public will be just so much the loser.... But while I freely admit all this, it yet remains true that a corporation which derives its powers from the State should pay to the State a just percentage of its earnings as a return for the privileges it enjoys."

This was quietly reasonable and uninflammatory doctrine. But the corporations would have none of it. The Republican machine, which had a majority in the Legislature, promptly repudiated it as well. The campaign contributions from the corporations were too precious to be jeopardized by legislation which the corporations did not want. The Governor argued, pleasantly and cheerfully. The organization balked sullenly. The corporations grinned knowingly. They had plenty of money with which to kill the bill, but they did not need to use it. The machine was working smoothly in their behalf. The bill was introduced and referred to a committee, and there it lay. No amount of argument and persuasion that the Governor could bring to bear availed to bring the bill out of hiding. So he sent in a special message, on almost the last day of the session. According to the rules of the New York Assembly, when the Governor sends in a special message on a given measure, the bill must be reported out and given consideration. But the machine was dazzled with its own arrogance. The Speaker would not have the message read. Some one actually tore it up.

This was more than a crime--it was a blunder. The wise ones in the organization realized it. They had no desire to have the Governor appeal to the people with his torn message in his hand. Roosevelt saw the error too, and laughed happily. He wrote another message and sent it over with the curt statement that, if it were not read forthwith, he would come over and read it himself. They knew that he would! So the Speaker read the message, and the bill was reported and hastily passed on the last day of the session.

Then the complacent corporations woke up. They had trusted the machine too far. What was more, they had underestimated the Governor's striking power. Now they came to him, hat in hand, and suggested some fault in the bill. He agreed with them. They asked if he would not call a special session to amend the bill. Again he agreed. The session was called, and the amendments were proposed. In addition, however, certain amendments that would have frustrated the whole purpose of the bill were suggested. The organization, still at its old tricks, tried to get back into its possession the bill already passed. But the Governor was not easily caught napping. He knew as well as they did that possession of the bill gave him the whip hand. He served notice that the second bill would contain precisely the amendments agreed upon and no others. Otherwise he would sign the first bill and let it become law, with all its imperfections on its head. Once more the organization and the corporations emulated Davy Crockett's coon and begged him not to shoot, for they would come down. The amended bill was passed and became law. But there was an epilogue to this little drama. The corporations proceeded to attack the constitutionality of the law on the ground of the very amendment for which they had so clamorously pleaded. But they failed. The Supreme Court of the United States, after Roosevelt had become President, affirmed the constitutionality of the law.

The spectacular events of Roosevelt's governorship were incidents in this conflict between two political philosophies, the one held by Platt and his tribe, the other by Roosevelt. Extracts from two letters exchanged by the Senator and the Governor bring the contrast between these philosophies into clear relief. Platt wrote as follows:

"When the subject of your nomination was under consideration, there was one matter that gave me real anxiety.... I had heard from a good many sources that you were a little loose on the relations of capital and labor, on trusts and combinations, and, indeed, on those numerous questions which have recently arisen in politics affecting the security of earnings and the right of a man to run his business in his own way, with due respect, of course, to the Ten Commandments and the Penal Code. Or, to get at it even more clearly, I understood from a number of business men, and among them many of your own personal friends, that you entertained various altruistic ideas, all very well in their way, but which before they could safely be put into law needed very profound consideration."[3]

Roosevelt replied that he had known very well that the Senator had just these feelings about him, and then proceeded to set forth his own view of the matter. With his usual almost uncanny wisdom in human relations, he based his argument on party expediency, which he knew Platt would comprehend, rather than on abstract considerations of right and wrong, in which realm the boss would be sure to feel rather at sea. He wrote thus:

"I know that when parties divide on such issues [as Bryanism] the tendency is to force everybody into one of two camps, and to throw out entirely men like myself, who are as strongly opposed to Populism in every stage as the greatest rep-

3  Roosevelt, "Autobiography"

resentative of corporate wealth but who also feel strongly that many of these representatives of enormous corporate wealth have themselves been responsible for a portion of the conditions against which Bryanism is in ignorant revolt. I do not believe that it is wise or safe for us as a party to take refuge in mere negation and to say that there are no evils to be corrected. It seems to me that our attitude should be one of correcting the evils and thereby showing that whereas the Populists, Socialists, and others do not correct the evils at all, or else do so at the expense of producing others in aggravated form, on the contrary we Republicans hold the just balance and set ourselves as resolutely against improper corporate influence on the one hand as against demagogy and mob rule on the other."[4]

This was the fight that Roosevelt was waging in every hour of his political career. It was a middle-of-the-road fight, not because of any timidity or slack-fibered thinking which prevented a committal to one extreme or the other, but because of a stern conviction that in the golden middle course was to be found truth and the right. It was an inevitable consequence that first one side and then the other--and sometimes both at once--should attack him as a champion of the other. It became a commonplace of his experience to be inveighed against by reformers as a reactionary and to be assailed by conservatives as a radical. But this paradoxical experience did not disturb him at all. He was concerned only to have the testimony of his own mind and conscience that he was right.

The contests which he had as Governor were spectacular and exhilarating; but they did not fill all the hours of his working days. A tremendous amount of spade work was actually accomplished. For example, he brought about the reenactment of the Civil Service Law, which under his predecessor had been repealed, and put through a mass of labor legislation for the betterment of conditions under which the workers carried on their daily lives. This legislation included laws to increase the number of factory inspectors, to create a tenement-house commission, to regulate sweatshop labor, to make the eight-hour and prevailing rate of wages law effective, to compel railways to equip freight trains with air brakes, to regulate the working hours of women, to protect women and children from dangerous machinery, to enforce good scaffolding provisions for workmen on buildings, to provide seats for the use of waitresses in hotels and restaurants, to reduce the hours of labor for drug-

---

4   Roosevelt, Autobiography

store clerks, to provide for the registration of laborers for municipal employment. He worked hard to secure an employers' liability law, but the time for this was not yet come.

Many of these reforms are now matters of course that no employer would think of attempting to eliminate. But they were new ideas then; and it took vision and courage to fight for them.

Roosevelt would have been glad to be elected Governor for a second term. But destiny, working through curious instruments, would not have it so. He left behind him in the Empire State, not only a splendid record of concrete achievement but something more than that. Jacob Riis has told how, some time after, an old State official at Albany, who had seen many Governors come and go, revealed this intangible something. Mr. Riis had said to him that he did not care much for Albany since Roosevelt had gone, and his friend replied: "Yes, we think so, many of us. The place seemed dreary when he was gone. But I know now that he left something behind that was worth our losing him to get. This past winter, for the first time, I heard the question spring up spontaneously, as it seemed, when a measure was up in the Legislature 'Is it right?' Not 'Is it expedient?' not 'How is it going to help me?' not 'What is it worth to the party?' Not any of these, but 'Is it right?' That is Roosevelt's legacy to Albany. And it was worth his coming and his going to have that."

# CHAPTER VI. ROOSEVELT BECOMES PRESIDENT

There was chance in Theodore Roosevelt's coming into the Presidency as he did, but there was irony as well. An evil chance dropped William McKinley before an assassin's bullet; but there was a fitting irony in the fact that the man who must step into his place had been put where he was in large measure by the very men who would least like to see him become President.

The Republican convention of 1900 was a singularly unanimous body. President McKinley was renominated without a murmur of dissent. But there was no Vice-President to renominate, as Mr. Hobart had died in office. There was no logical candidate for the second place on the ticket. Senator Platt, however, had a man whom he wanted to get rid of, since Governor Roosevelt had made himself persona non grata alike to the machine politicians of his State and to the corporations allied with them. The Governor, however, did not propose to be disposed of so easily. His reasons were characteristic. He wrote thus to Senator Platt about the matter:

"I can't help feeling more and more that the Vice-Presidency is not an office in which I could do anything and not an office in which a man who is still vigorous and not past middle life has much chance of doing anything.... Now, I should like to be Governor for another term, especially if we are able to take hold of the canals in serious shape. But, as Vice-President, I don't see there is anything I can do. I would be simply a presiding officer, and that I should find a bore."

Now Mr. Platt knew that nothing but "sidetracking" could stop another nomination of Roosevelt for the Governorship, and this Rough Rider was a thorn in his flesh. So he went on his subterranean way to have him nominated for the most innocuous political berth in the gift of the American people. He secured the cooperation of Senator Quay of Pennsylvania and another boss or two of the same indelible stripe; but all their political strength would not have accomplished the desired result without assistance from quite a different source. Roosevelt had already achieved great popularity in the Middle and the Far West for the very reasons which made Mr. Platt want him out of the way. So, while the New York boss and his acquiescent delegates were stopped from presenting his name to the convention by Roosevelt's assurance that he would fight a l'outrance any movement from his own State to nominate him, other delegates took matters into their own hands and the nomination was finally made unanimously.

Roosevelt gave great strength to the Republican ticket in the campaign which followed. William Jennings Bryan was again the Democratic candidate, but the "paramount issue" of his campaign had changed since four years before from free silver to anti-imperialism. President McKinley, according to his custom, made no active campaign; but Bryan and Roosevelt competed with each other in whirlwind speaking tours from one end of the country to the other. The war-cry of the Republicans was the "full dinner pail"; the keynote of Bryan's bid for popular support was opposition to the Republican policy of expansion and criticism of Republican tendencies toward plutocratic control. The success of the Republican ticket was overwhelming; McKinley and Roosevelt received nearly twice as many electoral votes as Bryan and Stevenson.

When President McKinley was shot at Buffalo six months after his second term began, it looked for a time as though he would recover. So Roosevelt, after an immediate visit to Buffalo, went to join his family in the Adirondacks. The news of the President's impending death found him out in the wilderness on the top of Mount Tahawus, not far from the tiny Lake Tear-of-the-Clouds, the source of the Hudson River. A ten-mile dash down the mountain trail, in the course of which he outstripped all his companions but one; a wild forty-mile drive through the night to the railroad, the new President and his single companion changing the horses two or three times with their own hands; a fast journey by special train across the State--and on the evening of September 14, 1901, Theodore Roosevelt took the oath of office as the twenty-sixth President of the United States.

Before taking the oath, Roosevelt announced that it would be his aim "to continue absolutely unbroken the policy of President McKinley for the peace, prosperity, and honor of our beloved country." He immediately asked every member of the late President's Cabinet to continue in office. The Cabinet was an excellent one, and

Mr. Roosevelt found it necessary to make no other changes than those that came in the ordinary course of events. The policies were not altered in broad general outline, for Roosevelt was as stalwart a Republican as McKinley himself, and was as firmly convinced of the soundness of the fundamentals of the Republican doctrine.

But the fears of some of his friends that Roosevelt would seem, if he carried out his purpose of continuity, "a pale copy of McKinley" were not justified in the event. They should have known better. A copy of any one Roosevelt could neither be nor seem, and "pale" was the last epithet to be applied to him with justice. It could not be long before the difference in the two Administrations would appear in unmistakable terms. The one which had just passed was first of all a party Administration and secondly a McKinley Administration. The one which followed was first, last, and all the time a Roosevelt Administration. "Where Macgregor sits, there is the head of the table." Not because Roosevelt consciously willed it so, but because the force and power and magnetism of his vigorous mind and personality inevitably made it so. McKinley had been a great harmonizer. "He oiled the machinery of government with loving and imperturbable patience," said an observer of his time, "and the wheels ran with an ease unknown since Washington's first term of office." It had been a constant reproach of the critics of the former President that "his ear was always to the ground." But he kept it there because it was his sincere conviction that it belonged there, ready to apprize him of the vibrations of the popular will. Roosevelt was the born leader with an innate instinct of command. He did not scorn or flout the popular will; he had too confirmed a conviction of the sovereign right of the people to rule for that. But he did not wait pusillanimously for the popular mind to make itself up; he had too high a conception of the duty of leadership for that. He esteemed it his peculiar function as the man entrusted by a great people with the headship of their common affairs--to lead the popular mind, to educate it, to inspire it, sometimes to run before it in action, serene in the confidence that tardy popular judgment would confirm the rightness of the deed.

By the end of Roosevelt's first Administration two of the three groups that had taken a hand in choosing him for the Vice-Presidency were thoroughly sick of their bargain. The machine politicians and the great corporations found that their cunning plan to stifle with the wet blanket of that depressing office the fires of his moral earnestness and pugnacious honesty had overreached itself. Fate had freed him and, once freed, he was neither to hold nor to bind. It was less than two years before Wall Street was convinced that he was "unsafe," and sadly shook its head over his "impetuosity." When Wall Street stamps a man "unsafe," the last word in condemnation has been said. It was an even shorter time before the politicians found him unsatisfactory. "The breach between Mr. Roosevelt and the politicians was, however, inevitable. His rigid insistence upon the maintenance and the extension of the merit system alone assured the discontent which precedes dislike," wrote another observer. "The era of patronage mongering in the petty offices ceased suddenly, and the spoilsmen had the right to say that in this respect the policy of McKinley had not been followed." It was true. When Roosevelt became President the civil service was thoroughly demoralized. Senators and Congressmen, by tacit agreement with the executive, used the appointing power for the payment of political debts, the reward of party services, the strengthening of their personal "fences." But within three months it was possible to say with absolute truth that "a marvelous change has already been wrought in the morale of the civil service." At the end of Roosevelt's first term an unusually acute and informed foreign journalist was moved to write, "No President has so persistently eliminated politics from his nominations, none has been more unbending in making efficiency his sole test."

There was the kernel of the whole matter: the President's insistence upon efficiency. Roosevelt, however, did not snatch rudely away from the Congressmen and Senators the appointing power which his predecessors had allowed them gradually to usurp. He continued to consult each member of the Congress upon appointments in that member's State or district and merely demanded that the men recommended for office should be honest, capable, and fitted for the places they were to fill.

President Roosevelt was not only ready and glad to consult with Senators but he sought and often took the advice of party leaders outside of Congress, and even took into consideration the opinions of bosses. In New York, for instance, the two Republican leaders, Governor Odell and Senator Platt, were sometimes in accord and sometimes in disagreement, but each was always desirous of being consulted. A letter written by Roosevelt in the middle of his first term to a friendly Congressman well illustrates his theory and practice in such cases:

"I want to work with Platt. I want to work with Odell. I want to support both and take the advice of both. But, of course, ultimately I must be the judge as to acting on the advice given. When, as in the case of the judgeship, I am convinced that the advice of both is wrong, I shall act as I did when I appointed Holt. When I can find a friend of Odell's like Cooley, who is thoroughly fit for the position I desire to fill, it gives me the greatest pleasure to appoint him. When Platt proposes to me a man like Hamilton Fish, it is equally a pleasure to appoint him."

This high-minded and common-sense course did not, however, seem to please the politicians, for dyed-in-the-wool politicians are curious persons to whom half a loaf is no consolation whatever, even when the other half of the loaf is to go to the people--without whom there would be no policies at all. Strangely enough, Roosevelt's policy was equally displeasing to those of the doctrinaire reformer type, to whom there is no word in the language more distasteful than "politician," unless it be the word "practical." But there was one class to whom the results of this common-sense brand of political action were eminently satisfactory, and this class made up the third group that had a part in the selection of Theodore Roosevelt for the Vice-Presidency. The plain people, especially in the more westerly portions of the country, were increasingly delighted with the honesty, the virility, and the effectiveness of the Roosevelt Administration. Just before the convention which was to nominate Roosevelt for the Presidency to succeed himself, an editorial writer expressed the fact thus: "The people at large are not oblivious of the fact that, while others are talking and carping, Mr. Roosevelt is carrying on in the White House a persistent and never-ending moral struggle with every powerful selfish and exploiting interest in the country."

Oblivious of it? They were acutely conscious of it. They approved of it with heartiness. They liked it so well that, when the time came to nominate and elect another President, they swept aside with a mighty rush not only the scruples and antagonisms of the Republican politicians and the "special interests" but party lines as well, and chose Roosevelt with a unanimous voice in the convention and a majority of two and a half million votes at the polls.

As President, Theodore Roosevelt achieved many concrete results. But his greatest contribution to the forward movement of the times was in the rousing of the public conscience, the strengthening of the nation's moral purpose, and the erecting of a new standard of public service in the management of the nation's affairs. It was no little thing that when Roosevelt was ready to hand over to another the responsibilities of his high office, James Bryce, America's best friend and keenest student from across the seas, was able to say that in a long life, during which he had studied intimately the government of many different countries, he had never in any country seen a more eager, high-minded, and efficient set of public servants, men more useful and more creditable to their country, than the men then doing the work of the American Government in Washington and in the field.

# CHAPTER VII. THE SQUARE DEAL FOR BUSINESS

During the times of Roosevelt, the American people were profoundly concerned with the trust problem. So was Roosevelt himself. In this important field of the relations between "big business" and the people he had a perfectly definite point of view, though he did not have a cut and dried programme. He was always more interested in a point of view than in a programme, for he realized that the one is lasting, the other shifting. He knew that if you stand on sound footing and look at a subject from the true angle, you may safely modify your plan of action as often and as rapidly as may be necessary to fit changing conditions. But if your footing is insecure or your angle of vision distorted, the most attractive programme in the world may come to ignominious disaster.

There were, broadly speaking, three attitudes toward the trust problem which were strongly held by different groups in the United States. At one extreme was the threatening growl of big business, "Let us alone!" At the other pole was the shrill outcry of William Jennings Bryan and his fellow exhorters, "Smash the trusts!" In the golden middle ground was the vigorous demand of Roosevelt for a "square deal."

In his first message to Congress, the President set forth his point of view with frankness and clarity. His comprehensive discussion of the matter may be summarized thus: The tremendous and highly complex industrial development which went on with great rapidity during the latter half of the nineteenth century produced serious social problems. The old laws and the old customs which had almost the binding force of law were once quite sufficient to regulate the accumulation and distribution of wealth. Since the industrial changes which have so enormously increased the productive power of mankind, these regulations are no longer sufficient. The process of the creation of great corporate fortunes has aroused much antagonism; but much of this, antagonism has been without warrant. There have been, it is true, abuses connected with the accumulation of wealth; yet no fortune can be accumulated in legitimate business except by conferring immense incidental benefits upon others. The men who have driven the great railways across the continent, who have built up commerce and developed manufactures, have on the whole done great good to the people at large. Without such men the material development of which Americans are so justly proud never could have taken place. They should therefore recognize the immense importance of this material development by leaving as unhampered as is compatible with the public good the strong men upon whom the success of business inevitably rests. It cannot too often be pointed out that to strike with ignorant violence at the interests of one set of men almost inevitably endangers the interests of all. The fundamental rule in American national life is that, on the whole and in the long run, we shall all go up or down together. Many of those who have made it their vocation to denounce the great industrial combinations appeal especially to the primitive instincts of hatred and fear. These are precisely the two emotions which unfit men for cool and steady judgment. The whole history of the world shows that legislation, in facing new industrial conditions, will generally be both unwise and ineffective unless it is undertaken only after calm inquiry and with sober self-restraint.

This is one side of the picture as it was presented by the President in his message to Congress. It was characteristic that this aspect should be put first, for Roosevelt always insisted upon doing justice to the other side before he demanded justice for his own. But he then proceeded to set forth the other side with equal vigor: There is a widespread conviction in the minds of the American people that the great corporations are in certain of their features and tendencies hurtful to the general welfare. It is true that real and grave evils have arisen, one of the chief of them being overcapitalization, with its many baleful consequences. This state of affairs demands that combination and concentration in business should be, not prohibited, but supervised and controlled. Corporations engaged in interstate commerce should be regulated if they are found to exercise a license working to the public injury. The first essential in determining how to deal with the great industrial combinations is knowledge of the facts. This is to be obtained only through publicity, which is the one sure remedy we can now invoke before it can be determined what further remedies are needed. Corporations should be subject to proper governmental supervision, and full and accurate information as to their operations should be made public at regular intervals. The nation should assume powers of supervision and regulation over all corporations doing an interstate business. This is especially true where the corporation derives a portion of its wealth from the existence of some monopolistic element or tendency in its business. The Federal Government should regulate the activities of corporations doing an interstate business, just as it regulates the activities of national banks, and, through the Interstate Commerce Commission, the operations of the railroads.

Roosevelt was destined, however, not to achieve the full measure of national control of corporations that he desired. The elements opposed to his view were too powerful. There was a fortuitous involuntary partnership though it was not admitted and was even violently denied between the advocates of "Let us alone!" and of "Smash the trusts!" against the champion of the middle way. In his "Autobiography" Roosevelt has described this situation:

"One of the main troubles was the fact that the men who saw the evils and who tried to remedy them attempted to work in two wholly different ways, and the great majority of them in a way that offered little promise of real betterment. They tried (by the Sherman law method) to bolster up an individualism already proved to be both futile and mischievous; to remedy by more individualism the concentration that was the inevitable result of the already existing individualism. They saw the evil done by the big combinations, and sought to remedy it by destroying them and restoring the country to the economic conditions of the middle of the nineteenth century. This was a hopeless effort, and those who went into it, although they regarded themselves as radical progressives, really represented a form of sincere rural toryism. They confounded monopolies with big business combinations, and in the effort to prohibit both alike, instead of where possible prohibiting one and drastically controlling the other, they succeeded merely in preventing any effective control of either.

"On the other hand, a few men recognized that corporations and combinations had become indispensable in the business world, that it was folly to try to prohibit them, but that it was also folly to leave them without thoroughgoing control. These men realized that the doctrine of the old laissez faire economists, of the believers in unlimited competition, unlimited individualism, were, in the actual state of affairs, false and mischievous. They realized that the Government must now interfere to protect labor, to subordinate the big corporation to the public welfare, and to shackle cunning and fraud exactly as centuries before it had interfered to shackle the physical force which does wrong by violence. The big reactionaries of the business world and their allies and instruments among politicians and newspaper editors took advantage of this division of opinion, and especially of the fact that most of their opponents were on the wrong path; and fought to keep matters absolutely unchanged. These men demanded for themselves an immunity from government control which, if granted, would have been as wicked and as foolish as immunity to the barons of the twelfth century. Many of them were evil men. Many others were just as good men as were some of these same barons; but they were as utterly unable as any medieval castle-owner to understand what the public interest really was. There have been aristocracies which have played a great and beneficent part at stages in the growth of mankind; but we had come to a stage where for our people what was needed was a real democracy; and of all forms of tyranny the least attractive and the most vulgar is the tyranny of mere wealth, the tyranny of a plutocracy."[5]

When Roosevelt became President, there were three directions in which energy needed to be applied to the solution of the trust problem: in the more vigorous enforcement of the laws already on the statute books; in the enactment of necessary new laws on various phases of the subject; and in the arousing of an intelligent and militant public opinion in relation to the whole question. To each of these purposes the new President applied himself with characteristic vigor.

The Sherman Anti-Trust law, which had already been on the Federal statute books for eleven years, forbade "combinations in restraint of trade" in the field of interstate commerce. During three administrations, eighteen actions had been brought by the Government for its enforcement. At the opening of the twentieth century it was a grave question whether the Sherman law was of any real efficacy in preventing the evils that arose from unregulated combination in business. A decision of the United States Supreme Court, rendered in 1895 in the so-called Knight case, against the American Sugar Refining Company, had, in the general belief, taken the teeth out of the Sherman law. In the words of Mr. Taft, "The effect of

---

5  Autobiography

the decision in the Knight case upon the popular mind, and indeed upon Congress as well, was to discourage hope that the statute could be used to accomplish its manifest purpose and curb the great industrial trusts which, by the acquisition of all or a large percentage of the plants engaged in the manufacture of a commodity, by the dismantling of some and regulating the output of others, were making every effort to restrict production, control prices, and monopolize the business." It was obviously necessary that the Sherman act, unless it were to pass into innocuous desuetude, should have the original vigor intended by Congress restored to it by a new interpretation of the law on the part of the Supreme Court. Fortunately an opportunity for such a change presented itself with promptness. A small group of powerful financiers had arranged to take control of practically the entire system of railways in the Northwest, "possibly," Roosevelt has said, "as the first step toward controlling the entire railway system of the country." They had brought this about by organizing the Northern Securities Company to hold the majority of the stock of two competing railways, the Great Northern and the Northern Pacific. At the direction of President Roosevelt, suit was brought by the Government to prevent the merger. The defendants relied for protection upon the immunity afforded by the decision in the Knight case. But the Supreme Court now took more advanced ground, decreed that the Northern Securities Company was an illegal combination, and ordered its dissolution.

By the successful prosecution of this case the Sherman act was made once more a potentially valuable instrument for the prevention of the more flagrant evils that flow from "combinations in restraint of trade." During the remaining years of the Roosevelt Administrations, this legal instrument was used with aggressive force for the purpose for which it was intended. In seven years and a half, forty-four prosecutions were brought under it by the Government, as compared with eighteen in the preceding eleven years. The two most famous trust cases, next to the Northern Securities case and even surpassing it in popular interest, because of the stupendous size of the corporations involved, were those against the Standard Oil Company and the American Tobacco Company. These companion cases were not finally decided in the Supreme Court until the Administration of President Taft; but their prosecution was begun while Roosevelt was in office and by his direction. They were therefore a definite part of his campaign for the solution of the vexed trust problem.

Both cases were decided, by every court through which they passed, in favor of the Government. The Supreme Court finally in 1911 decreed that both the Standard Oil and the Tobacco trusts were in violation of the Sherman act and ordered their dissolution. There could now no longer be any question that the Government could in fact exercise its sovereign will over even the greatest and the most powerful of modern business organizations.

The two cases had one other deep significance which at first blush looked like a weakening of the force of the anti-trust law but which was in reality a strengthening of it. There had been long and ardent debate whether the Sherman act should be held to apply to all restraints of trade or only to such as were unreasonable. It was held by some that it applied to ALL restraints and therefore should be amended to cover only unreasonable restraints. It was held by others that it applied to all restraints and properly so. It was held by still others that it applied only to unreasonable restraints. But the matter had never been decided by competent authority. The decision of the Supreme Court in these two outstanding cases, however, put an end to the previous uncertainty. Chief Justice White, in his two opinions, laid it down with definiteness that in construing and applying the law recourse must be had to the "rule of reason." He made clear the conviction of the court that it was "undue" restraints of trade which the law forbade and not incidental or inconsiderable ones. This definitive interpretation of the law, while it caused considerable criticism at the moment, in ultimate effect so cleared the air about the Sherman act as effectually to dispose of the demands for its amendment in the direction of greater leniency or severity.

But the proving of the anti-trust law as an effective weapon against the flagrantly offending trusts, according to Roosevelt's conviction, was only a part of the battle. As he said, "monopolies can, although in rather cumbrous fashion, be broken up by lawsuits. Great business combinations, however, cannot possibly be made useful instead of noxious industrial agencies merely by lawsuits, and especially by lawsuits supposed to be carried on for their destruction and not for their control and regulation." He took, as usual, the constructive point of view. He saw both sides of the trust question--the inevitability and the beneficence of combination in modern business, and the danger to the public good that lay in the unregulated and uncontrolled wielding of great power by private individuals. He believed that the thing to do with great power was not to destroy it but to use it, not to forbid its acquisition but to direct its application. So he set himself to the task of securing fresh legislation regarding the regulation of corporate activities.

Such legislation was not easy to get; for the forces of reaction were strong in Congress. But several significant steps in this direction were taken before Roosevelt went out of office. The new Federal Department of Commerce and Labor was created, and its head became a member of the Cabinet. The Bureau of Corporations was established in the same department. These new executive agencies were given no regulatory powers, but they did perform excellent service in that field of publicity on the value of which Roosevelt laid so much stress.

In the year 1906 the passing of the Hepburn railway rate bill for the first time gave the Interstate Commerce Commission a measure of real control over the railways, by granting to the Commission the power to fix maximum rates for the transportation of freight in interstate commerce. The Commission had in previous years, under the authority of the act which created it and which permitted the Commission to decide in particular cases whether rates were just and reasonable, attempted to exercise this power to fix in these specific cases maximum rates. But the courts had decided that the Commission did not possess this right. The Hepburn act also extended the authority of the Commission over express companies, sleeping-car companies, pipe lines, private car lines, and private terminal and connecting lines. It prohibited railways from transporting in interstate commerce any commodities produced or owned by themselves. It abolished free passes and transportation except for railway employees and certain other small classes of persons, including the poor and unfortunate classes and those engaged in religious and charitable work. Under the old law, the Commission was compelled to apply to a Federal court on its own initiative for the enforcement of any order which it might issue. Under the Hepburn act the order went into effect at once; the railroad must begin to obey the order within thirty days; it must itself appeal to the court for the suspension and revocation of the order, or it must suffer a penalty of $5000 a day during the time that the order was disobeyed. The act further gave the Commission the power to prescribe accounting methods which must be followed by the railways, in order to make more difficult the concealment of illegal rates and improper favors to individual shippers. This extension and strengthening of the authority of the Interstate Commerce Commission was an extremely valuable forward step, not only as concerned the relations of the public and the railways, but in connection with the development of predatory corporations of the Standard Oil type. Miss Ida Tarbell, in her frankly revealing "History of the Standard Oil Company", which had been published in 1904, had shown in striking fashion how secret concessions from the railways had helped to build up that great structure of business monopoly. In Miss Tarbell's words, "Mr. Rockefeller's great purpose had been made possible by his remarkable manipulation of the railroads. It was the rebate which had made the Standard Oil trust, the rebate, amplified, systematized, glorified into a power never equalled before or since by any business of the country." The rebate was the device by which favored shippers--favored by the railways either voluntarily or under the compulsion of the threats of retaliation which the powerful shippers were able to make--paid openly the established freight rates on their products and then received back from the railways a substantial proportion of the charges. The advantage to the favored shipper is obvious. There were other more adroit ways in which the favoritism could be accomplished; but the general principle was the same. It was one important purpose--and effect--of the Hepburn act to close the door to this form of discrimination.

One more step was necessary in order to eradicate completely this mischievous condition and to "keep the highway of commerce open to all on equal terms." It was imperative that the law relative to these abuses should be enforced. On this point Roosevelt's own words are significant: "Although under the decision of the courts the National Government had power over the railways, I found, when I became President, that this power was either not exercised at all or exercised with utter inefficiency. The law against rebates was a dead letter. All the unscrupulous railway men had been allowed to violate it with impunity; and because of this, as was inevitable, the scrupulous and decent railway men had been forced to violate it themselves, under penalty of being beaten by their less scrupulous rivals. It was not the fault of these decent railway men. It was the fault of the Government."

Roosevelt did not propose that this condition should continue to be the fault of the Government while he was at its head, and he inaugurated a vigorous campaign against railways that had given rebates and against corporations that had accepted-- or extorted-them. The campaign reached a spectacular peak in a prosecution of the

Standard Oil Company, in which fines aggregating over $29,000,000 were imposed by Judge Kenesaw M. Landis of the United States District Court at Chicago for the offense of accepting rebates. The Circuit Court of Appeals ultimately determined that the fine was improperly large, since it had been based on the untenable theory that each shipment on which a rebate was paid constituted a separate offense. At the second trial the presiding judge ordered an acquittal. In spite, however, of the failure of this particular case, with its spectacular features, the net result of the rebate prosecutions was that the rebate evil was eliminated for good and all from American railway and commercial life.

When Roosevelt demanded the "square deal" between business and the people, he meant precisely what he said. He had no intention of permitting justice to be required from the great corporations without insisting that justice be done to them in turn. The most interesting case in point was that of the Tennessee Coal and Iron Company. To this day the action which Roosevelt took in the matter is looked upon, by many of those extremists who can see nothing good in "big business," as a proof of his undue sympathy with the capitalist. But thirteen years later the United States Supreme Court in deciding the case against the United States Steel Corporation in favor of the Corporation, added an obiter dictum which completely justified Roosevelt's action.

In the fall of 1907 the United States was in the grip of a financial panic. Much damage was done, and much more was threatened. One great New York trust company was compelled to close its doors, and others were on the verge of disaster. One evening in the midst of this most trying time, the President was informed that two representatives of the United States Steel Corporation wished to call upon him the next morning. As he was at breakfast the next day word came to him that Judge Gary and Mr. Frick were waiting in the Executive Office. The President went over at once, sending word to Elihu Root, then Secretary of State, to join him. Judge Gary and Mr. Frick informed the President that a certain great firm in the New York financial district was upon the point of failure. This firm held a large quantity of the stock of the Tennessee Coal and Iron Company. The Steel Corporation had been urged to purchase this stock in order to avert the failure. The heads of the Steel Corporation asserted that they did not wish to purchase this stock from the point of view of a business transaction, as the value which the property might be to the

Corporation would be more than offset by the criticism to which they would be subjected. They said that they were sure to be charged with trying to secure a monopoly and to stifle competition. They told the President that it had been the consistent policy of the Steel Corporation to have in its control no more than sixty per cent of the steel properties of the country; that their proportion of those properties was in fact somewhat less than sixty per cent; and that the acquisition of the holdings of the Tennessee Company would raise it only a little above that point. They felt, however, that it would be extremely desirable for them to make the suggested purchase in order to prevent the damage which would result from the failure of the firm in question. They were willing to buy the stocks offered because in the best judgment of many of the strongest bankers in New York the transaction would be an influential factor in preventing a further extension of the panic. Judge Gary and Mr. Frick declared that they were ready to make the purchase with this end in view but that they would not act without the President's approval of their action.

Immediate action was imperative. It was important that the purchase, if it were to be made, should be announced at the opening of the New York Stock Exchange at ten o'clock that morning. Fortunately Roosevelt never shilly-shallied when a crisis confronted him. His decision was instantaneous. He assured his callers that while, of course, he could not advise them to take the action, proposed, he felt that he had no public duty to interpose any objection.

This assurance was quite sufficient. The pure chase was made and announced, the firm in question did not fail, and the panic was arrested. The immediate reaction of practically the whole country was one of relief. It was only later, when the danger was past, that critics began to make themselves heard. Any one who had taken the trouble to ascertain the facts would have known beyond question that the acquisition of the Tennessee properties was not sufficient to change the status of the Steel Corporation under the anti-trust law. But the critics did not want to know the facts. They wanted--most of them, at least--to have a stick with which to beat Roosevelt. Besides, many of them did not hold Roosevelt's views about the square deal. Their belief was that whatever big business did was ipso facto evil and that it was the duty of public officials to find out what big business wanted to do and then prevent its accomplishment.

Under a later Administration, Roosevelt was invited to come before a Congressional investigating committee to explain what he did in this famous case. There he told the complete story of the occurrence simply, frankly, and emphatically, and ended with this statement: "If I were on a sailboat, I should not ordinarily meddle with any of the gear; but if a sudden squall struck us, and the main sheet jammed, so that the boat threatened to capsize, I would unhesitatingly cut the main sheet, even though I were sure that the owner, no matter how grateful to me at the moment for having saved his life, would a few weeks later, when he had forgotten his danger and his fear, decide to sue me for the value of the cut rope. But I would feel a hearty contempt for the owner who so acted."

Two laws passed during the second Roosevelt Administration had an important bearing on the conduct of American business, though in a different way from those which have already been considered. They were the Pure Food law, and the Meat Inspection act. Both were measures for the protection of the public health; but both were at the same time measures for the control of private business. The Pure Food law did three things: it prohibited the sale of foods or drugs which were not pure and unadulterated; it prohibited the sale of drugs which contained opium, cocaine, alcohol, and other narcotics unless the exact proportion of them in the preparation were stated on the package; and it prohibited the sale of foods and drugs as anything else than what they actually were. The Meat Inspection law required rigid inspection by Government officials of all slaughterhouses and packing concerns preparing meat food products for distribution in interstate commerce. The imperative need for the passage of this law was brought forcibly and vividly to the popular attention through a novel, "The Jungle", written by Upton Sinclair, in which the disgraceful conditions of uncleanliness and revolting carelessness in the Chicago packing houses were described with vitriolic intensity. An official investigation ordered by the President confirmed the truth of these timely revelations.

These achievements on the part of the Roosevelt Administrations were of high value. But, after all Roosevelt performed an even greater service in arousing the public mind to a realization of facts of national significance and stimulating the public conscience to a desire to deal with them vigorously and justly. From the very beginning of his Presidential career he realized the gravity of the problems created by the rise of big business; and he began forthwith to impress upon the people with hammer blows the conditions as he saw them, the need for definite corrective action, and the absolute necessity for such treatment of the case as would constitute the "square deal." An interesting example of his method and of the response which it received is to be found in the report of an address which he made in 1907. It runs thus:

"From the standpoint of our material prosperity there is only one other thing as important as the discouragement of a spirit of envy and hostility toward business men, toward honest men of means; this is the discouragement of dishonest business men. [Great applause.]

"Wait a moment; I don't want you to applaud this part unless you are willing to applaud also the part I read first, to which you listened in silence. [Laughter and applause.] I want you to understand that I will stand just as straight for the rights of the honest man who wins his fortune by honest methods as I will stand against the dishonest man who wins a fortune by dishonest methods. And I challenge the right to your support in one attitude just as much as in the other. I am glad you applauded when you did, but I want you to go back now and applaud the other statement. I will read a little of it over again. 'Every manifestation of ignorant envy and hostility toward honest men who acquire wealth by honest means should be crushed at the outset by the weight of a sensible public opinion.' [Tremendous applause.] Thank you. Now I'll go on."

Roosevelt's incessant emphasis was placed upon conduct as the proper standard by which to judge the actions of men. "We are," he once said, "no respecters of persons. If a labor union does wrong, we oppose it as firmly as we oppose a corporation which does wrong; and we stand equally stoutly for the rights of the man of wealth and for the rights of the wage-worker. We seek to protect the property of every man who acts honestly, of every corporation that represents wealth honestly accumulated and honestly used. We seek to stop wrongdoing, and we desire to punish the wrongdoer only so far as is necessary to achieve this end."

At another time he sounded the same note--sounded it indeed with a "damnable iteration" that only proved how deeply it was imbedded in his conviction.

"Let us strive steadily to secure justice as between man and man without regard to the man's position, social or otherwise. Let us remember that justice can never be justice unless it is equal. Do justice to the rich man and exact justice from him; do justice to the poor man and exact justice from him--justice to the capitalist and justice to the wage-worker.... I have an equally hearty aversion for the reactionary and the demagogue; but I am not going to be driven out of fealty to my principles because certain of them are championed by the reactionary and certain others by the demagogue. The reactionary is always strongly for the rights of property; so am I.... I will not be driven away from championship of the rights of property upon which all our civilization rests because they happen to be championed by people who champion furthermore the abuses of wealth.... Most demagogues advocate some excellent popular principles, and nothing could be more foolish than for decent men to permit themselves to be put into an attitude of ignorant and perverse opposition to all reforms demanded in the name of the people because it happens that some of them are demanded by demagogues."

Such an attitude on the part of a man like Roosevelt could not fail to be misunderstood, misinterpreted, and assailed. Toward the end of his Presidential career, when he was attacking with peculiar vigor the "malefactors of great wealth" whom the Government had found it necessary to punish for their predatory acts in corporate guise, it was gently intimated by certain defenders of privilege that he was insane. At other times, when he was insisting upon justice even to men who had achieved material success, he was placed by the more rabid of the radical opponents of privilege in the hierarchy of the worshipers of the golden calf. His course along the middle of the onward way exposed him peculiarly to the missiles of invective and scorn from the partisans on either side. But neither could drive him into the arms of the other.

The best evidence of the soundness of the strategy with which he assailed the enemies of the common good, with whirling war-club but with scrupulous observance of the demands of justice and fair play, is to be found in the measure of what he actually achieved. He did arouse the popular mind and sting the popular conscience broad awake. He did enforce the law without fear or favor. He did leave upon the statute-book and in the machinery of government new means and methods for the control of business and for the protection of the general welfare against predatory wealth.

# CHAPTER VIII. THE SQUARE DEAL FOR LABOR

It should go without saying that Roosevelt was vigorously and deeply concerned with the relations between capital and labor, for he was interested in everything that concerned the men and women of America, everything that had to do with human relations. From the very beginning of his public life he had been a champion of the workingman when the workingman needed defense against exploitation and injustice. But his advocacy of the workers' rights was never demagogic nor partial. In industrial relations, as in the relations between business and the community, he believed in the square deal. The rights of labor and the rights of capital must, he firmly held, be respected each by the other--and the rights of the public by both.

Roosevelt believed thoroughly in trade unions. He realized that one of the striking accompaniments of the gigantic developments in business and industry of the past few generations was a gross inequality in the bargaining relation between the employer and the individual employee standing alone.

Speaking of the great coal strike which occurred while he was President, he developed the idea in this way:

"The great coal-mining and coal-carrying companies, which employed their tens of thousands, could easily dispense with the services of any particular miner. The miner, on the other hand, however expert, could not dispense with the companies. He needed a job; his wife and children would starve if he did not get one. What the miner had to sell--his labor--was a perishable commodity; the labor of today--if not sold today was lost forever. Moreover, his labor was not like most commodities--a mere thing; it was a part of a living, human being. The workman saw, and all citizens who gave earnest thought to the matter saw that the labor problem was not only an economic, but also a moral, a human problem. Individually the miners were impotent when they sought to enter a wage contract with the great companies; they could make fair terms only by uniting into trade unions to bargain collectively. The men were forced to cooperate to secure not only their economic, but their simple human rights. They, like other workmen, were compelled by the very conditions under which they lived to unite in unions of their industry or trade, and those unions were bound to grow in size, in strength, and in power for good and evil as the industries in which the men were employed grew larger and larger."[6]

He was fond of quoting three statements of Lincoln's as expressing precisely what he himself believed about capital and labor. The first of these sayings was this: "Labor is prior to, and independent of, capital. Capital is only the fruit of labor, and could never have existed if labor had not first existed. Labor is the superior of capital, and deserves much the higher consideration."

This statement, Roosevelt used to say, would have made him, if it had been original with him, even more strongly denounced as a communist agitator than he already was! Then he would turn from this, which the capitalist ought to hear, to another saying of Lincoln's which the workingman ought to hear: "Capital has its rights, which are as worthy of protection as any other rights.. ... Nor should this lead to a war upon the owners of property. Property is the fruit of labor;... property is desirable; it is a positive good in the world."

Then would come the final word from Lincoln, driven home by Roosevelt with all his usual vigor and fire: "Let not him who is houseless pull down the house of another, but let him work diligently and build one for himself, thus by example assuring that his own shall be safe from violence when built."

In these three sayings, Roosevelt declared, Lincoln "showed the proper sense of proportion in his relative estimates of capital and labor, of human rights and property rights." Roosevelt's own most famous statement of the matter was made in an address which he delivered before the Sorbonne in Paris, on his way back from Africa: "In every civilized society property rights must be carefully safeguarded. Ordinarily, and in the great majority of cases, human rights and property rights are fundamentally and in the long run identical; but when it clearly appears that there is a real conflict between them, human rights must have the upper hand, for property belongs to man and not man to property."

---

6  Autobiography

Several times it happened to Roosevelt to be confronted with the necessity of meeting with force the threat of violence on the part of striking workers. He never refused the challenge, and his firmness never lost him the respect of any but the worthless among the workingmen. When he was Police Commissioner, strikers in New York were coming into continual conflict with the police. Roosevelt asked the strike leaders to meet him in order to talk things over. These leaders did not know the man with whom they were dealing; they tried to bully him. They truculently announced the things that they would do if the police were not compliant to their wishes. But they did not get far in that direction. Roosevelt called a halt with a snap of his jaws. "Gentlemen!" he said, "we want to understand one another. That was my object in coming here. Remember, please, that he who counsels violence does the cause of labor the poorest service. Also, he loses his case. Understand distinctly that order will be kept. The police will keep it. Now, gentlemen!" There was surprised silence for a moment, and then smashing applause. They had learned suddenly what kind of a man Roosevelt was. All their respect was his.

It was after he became President that his greatest opportunity occurred to put into effect his convictions about the industrial problem. In 1909. there was a strike which brought about a complete stoppage of work for several months in the anthracite coal regions. Both operators and workers were determined to make no concession. The coal famine became a national menace as the winter approached. "The big coal operators had banded together," so Roosevelt has described the situation, "and positively refused to take any steps looking toward an accommodation. They knew that the suffering among the miners was great; they were confident that if order was kept, and nothing further done by the Government, they would win; and they refused to consider that the public had any rights in the matter."

As the situation grew more and more dangerous, the President directed the head of the Federal Labor Bureau to make an investigation of the whole matter. From this investigation it appeared that the most feasible solution of the problem was to prevail upon both sides to agree to a commission of arbitration and promise to accept its findings. To this proposal the miners agreed; the mine owners insolently declined it. Nevertheless, Roosevelt persisted, and ultimately the operators yielded on condition that the commission, which was to be named by the President, should contain no representative of labor. They insisted that it should be composed of (1) an officer of the engineer corps of the army or navy, (2) a man with experience in mining, (3) a "man of prominence, eminent as a sociologist," (4) a Federal Judge of the Eastern District of Pennsylvania, and (5) a mining engineer. In the course of a long and grueling conference it looked as though a deadlock could be the only outcome, since the mine owners would have no representative of labor on any terms. But it suddenly dawned on Roosevelt that the owners were objecting not to the thing but to the name. He discovered that they would not object to the appointment of any man, labor man or not, so long as he was not appointed as a labor man or as a representative of labor. "I shall never forget," he says in his "Autobiography", "the mixture of relief and amusement I felt when I thoroughly grasped the fact that while they would heroically submit to anarchy rather than have Tweedledum, yet if I would call it Tweedledee they would accept with rapture." All that he needed to do was to "commit a technical and nominal absurdity with a solemn face." When he realized that this was the case, Roosevelt announced that he was glad to accept the terms laid down, and proceeded to appoint to the third position on the Commission the labor man whom he had wanted from the first to appoint, Mr. E. E. Clark, the head of the Brotherhood of Railway Conductors. He called him, however, an "eminent sociologist," adding in his announcement of the appointment this explanation: "For the purposes of such a Commission, the term sociologist means a man who has thought and studied deeply on social questions and has practically applied his knowledge."

The Commission as finally constituted was an admirable one. Its report, which removed every menace to peace in the coal industry, was an outstanding event in the history of the relations of labor and capital in the United States.

But the most interesting and significant part of Roosevelt's relation to the great coal strike concerned something that did not happen. It illustrates his habit of seeing clearly through a situation to the end and knowing far in advance just what action he was prepared to take in any contingency that might possibly arise. He was determined that work should be resumed in the mines and that the country should have coal. He did not propose to allow the operators to maintain the deadlock by sheer refusal to make any compromise. In case he could not succeed in making them reconsider their position, he had prepared a definite and drastic course of action. The facts in regard to this plan did not become public until many years after the strike was settled, and then only when Roosevelt described it in his "Autobiography".

The method of action which Roosevelt had determined upon in the last resort was to get the Governor of Pennsylvania to appeal to him as President to restore order. He had then determined to put Federal troops into the coal fields under the command of some first-rate general, with instructions not only to preserve order but to dispossess the mine operators and to run the mines as a receiver, until such time as the Commission should make its report and the President should issue further orders in view of that report. Roosevelt found an army officer with the requisite good sense, judgment, and nerve to act in such a crisis in the person of Major General Schofield. Roosevelt sent for the General and explained the seriousness of the crisis. "He was a fine fellow," says Roosevelt in his "Autobiography", "a most respectable-looking old boy, with side whiskers and a black skull-cap, without any of the outward aspect of the conventional military dictator; but in both nerve and judgment he was all right." Schofield quietly assured the President that if the order was given he would take possession of the mines, and would guarantee to open them and run them without permitting any interference either by the owners or by the strikers or by any one else, so long as the President told him to stay. Fortunately Roosevelt's efforts to bring about arbitration were ultimately successful and recourse to the novel expedient of having the army operate the coal mines proved unnecessary. No one was more pleased than Roosevelt himself at the harmonious adjustment of the trouble, for, as he said, "It is never well to take drastic action if the result can be achieved with equal efficiency in less drastic fashion." But there can be no question that the drastic action would have followed if the coal operators had not seen the light when they did.

In other phases of national life Roosevelt made his influence equally felt. As President he found that there was little which the Federal Government could do directly for the practical betterment of living and working conditions among the mass of the people compared with what the State Governments could do. He determined, however, to strive to make the National Government an ideal employer. He hoped to make the Federal employee feel, just as much as did the Cabinet officer, that he was one of the partners engaged in the service of the public, proud of his work, eager to do it efficiently, and confident of just treatment. The Federal Government could act in relation to laboring conditions only in the Territories, in the District of Columbia, and in connection with interstate commerce. But in those fields it accomplished much.

The eight-hour law for workers in the executive departments had become a mere farce and was continually violated by officials who made their subordinates work longer hours than the law stipulated. This condition the President remedied by executive action, at the same time seeing to it that the shirk and the dawdler received no mercy. A good law protecting the lives and health of miners in the Territories was passed; and laws were enacted for the District of Columbia, providing for the supervision of employment agencies, for safeguarding workers against accidents, and for the restriction of child labor. A workmen's compensation law for government employees, inadequate but at least a beginning, was put on the statute books. A similar law for workers on interstate railways was declared unconstitutional by the courts; but a second law was passed and stood the test.

It was chiefly in the field of executive action, however, that Roosevelt was able to put his theories into practice. There he did not have to deal with recalcitrant, stupid, or medieval-minded politicians, as he so often did in matters of legislation. One case which confronted him found him on the side against the labor unions, but, being sure that he was right, he did not let that fact disturb him. A printer in the Government Printing Office, named Miller, had been discharged because he was a non-union man. The President immediately ordered him reinstated.

Samuel Gompers, President of the American Federation of Labor, with several members of its Executive Council, called upon him to protest. The President was courteous but inflexible. He answered their protest by declaring that, in the employment and dismissal of men in the Government service, he could no more recognize the fact that a man did or did not belong to a union as being for or against him, than he could recognize the fact that he was a Protestant or a Catholic, a Jew or a Gentile, as being for or against him. He declared his belief in trade unions and said that if he were a worker himself he would unquestionably join a union. He always preferred to see a union shop. But he could not allow his personal preferences to control his public actions. The Government was bound to treat union and non-union men exactly alike. His action in causing Miller to be reinstated was final.

Another instance which illustrated Roosevelt's skill in handling a difficult situation occurred in 1908 when the Louisville and Nashville Railroad and certain other lines announced a reduction in wages. The heads of that particular road laid the necessity for the reduction at the door of "the drastic laws inimical to the interests of the railroads that have in the past year or two been enacted." A general strike, with all the attendant discomfort and disorder, was threatened in retaliation. The President wrote a letter to the Interstate Commerce Commission, in which he said:

"These reductions in wages may be justified or they may not. As to this the public, which is a vitally interested party, can form no judgment without a more complete knowledge of the essential facts and real merits of the case than it now has or than it can possibly obtain from the special pleadings, certain to be put forth by each side in case their dispute should bring about serious interruption to traffic. If the reduction in wages is due to natural causes, the loss of business being such that the burden should be, and is, equitably distributed, between capitalist and wageworker, the public should know it. If it is caused by legislation, the public and Congress should know it; and if it is caused by misconduct in the past financial or other operations of any railroad, then everybody should know it, especially if the excuse of unfriendly legislation is advanced as a method of covering up past business misconduct by the railroad managers, or as a justification for failure to treat fairly the wage-earning employees of the company."

The letter closed with a request to the Commission to investigate the whole matter with these points in view. But the investigation proved unnecessary; the letter was enough. The proposed reduction of wages was never heard of again. The strength of the President's position in a case of this sort was that he was cheerfully prepared to accept whatever an investigation should show to be right. If the reduction should prove to be required by natural causes, very well--let the reduction be made. If it was the result of unfair and unwise legislation, very well--repeal the legislation. If it was caused by misconduct on the part of railroad managers, very well--let them be punished. It was hard to get the better of a man who wanted only the truth, and was ready to act upon it, no matter which way it cut.

In 1910, after his return from Africa, a speaking trip happened to take him to Columbus, Ohio, which had for months been in the grasp of a street railway strike. There had been much violence, many policemen had refused to do their duty, and many officials had failed in theirs. It was an uncomfortable time for an outsider to come and make a speech. But Roosevelt did not dodge. He spoke, and straight to the point. His speech had been announced as on Law and Order. When he rose to speak, however, he declared that he would speak on Law, Order, and Justice. Here are some of the incisive things that he said:

"Now, the first requisite is to establish order; and the first duty of every official, in State and city alike, high and low, is to see that order obtains and that violence is definitely stopped .... I have the greatest regard for the policeman who does his duty. I put him high among the props of the State, but the policeman who mutinies, or refuses to perform his duty, stands on a lower level than that of the professional lawbreaker.... I ask, then, not only that civic officials perform their duties, but that you, the people, insist upon their performing them... . I ask this particularly of the wage-workers, and employees, and men on strike.... I ask them, not merely passively, but actively, to aid in restoring order. I ask them to clear their skirts of all suspicion of sympathizing with disorder, and, above all, the suspicion of sympathizing with those who commit brutal and cowardly assaults.... What I have said of the laboring men applies just as much to the capitalists and the capitalists' representatives.... The wage-workers and the representatives of the companies should make it evident that they wish the law absolutely obeyed; that there is no chance of saying that either the labor organization or the corporation favors lawbreakers or lawbreaking. But let your public servants trust, not in the good will of either side, but in the might of the civil arm, and see that law rules, that order obtains, and that every miscreant, every scoundrel who seeks brutally to assault any other man-- whatever that man's status--is punished with the utmost severity.... When you have obtained law and order, remember that it is useless to have obtained them unless upon them you build a superstructure of justice. After finding out the facts, see that justice is done; see that injustice that has been perpetrated in the past is remedied, and see that the chance of doing injustice in the future is minimized."

Now, any one might in his closet write an essay on Law, Order, and Justice, which would contain every idea that is here expressed. The essayist might even feel somewhat ashamed of his production on the ground that all the ideas that it contained were platitudes. But it is one thing to write an essay far from the madding crowd, and it was quite another to face an audience every member of which was probably a partisan of either the workers, the employers, or the officials, and give them straight from the shoulder simple platitudinous truths of this sort applicable to the situation in which they found themselves. Any one of them would have been delighted to hear these things said about his opponents; it was when they were addressed to himself and his associates that they stung. The best part of it, however, was the fact that those things were precisely what the situation needed. They were the truth; and Roosevelt knew it. His sword had a double edge, and he habitually used it with a sweep that cut both ways. As a result he was generally hated or feared by the extremists on both sides. But the average citizen heartily approved the impartiality of his strokes.

In the year 1905 the Governor of Idaho was killed by a bomb as he was leaving his house. A former miner, who had been driven from the State six years before by United States troops engaged in putting down industrial disorder, was arrested and confessed the crime. In his confession he implicated three officers of the Western Federation of Miners, Moyer, Haywood, and Pettibone. These three men were brought from Colorado into Idaho by a method that closely resembled kidnaping, though it subsequently received the sanction of the United States Supreme Court. While these prominent labor leaders were awaiting trial, Colorado, Idaho, and Nevada seethed and burst into eruption. Parts of the mining districts were transformed into two hostile armed camps. Violence was common. At this time Roosevelt coupled the name of a giant among American railroad financiers, with those of Moyer and Haywood, and described them all as "undesirable citizens." The outbursts of resentment from both sides were instantaneous and vicious. There was little to choose between them. Finally the President took advantage of a letter of criticism from a supporter of the accused labor leaders to reply to both groups of critics. He referred to the fact that certain representatives of the great capitalists had protested, because he had included a prominent financier with Moyer and Haywood, while certain representatives of labor had protested on precisely the opposite grounds. Then Roosevelt went on to say:

"I am as profoundly indifferent to the condemnation in one case as in the other. I challenge as a right the support of all good Americans, whether wage-workers or capitalists, whatever their occupation or creed, or in whatever portion of the country they live, when I condemn both the types of bad citizenship which I have held up to reprobation.... You ask for a 'square deal' for Messrs. Moyer and Haywood. So do I. When I say 'square deal', I mean a square deal to every one; it is equally a violation of the policy of the square deal for a capitalist to protest against denunciation of a capitalist who is guilty of wrongdoing and for a labor leader to protest against the denunciation of a labor leader who has been guilty of wrongdoing. I stand for equal justice to both; and so far as in my power lies I shall uphold justice, whether the man accused of guilt has behind him the wealthiest corporation, the greatest aggregations of riches in the country, or whether he has behind him the most influential labor organizations in the country."

It should be recorded for the sake of avoiding misapprehension that Roosevelt's denunciation of Moyer and Haywood was not based on the assumption that they were guilty of the death of the murdered' Governor, but was predicated on their general attitude and conduct in the industrial conflicts in the mining fields.

The criticisms of Roosevelt because of his actions in the complex relations of capital and labor were often puerile. For instance, he was sternly taken to task on one or two occasions because he had labor leaders lunch with him at the White House. He replied to one of his critics with this statement of his position: "While I am President I wish the labor man to feel that he has the same right of access to me that the capitalist has; that the doors swing open as easily to the wageworker as to the head of a big corporation--AND NO EASIER."

# CHAPTER IX. RECLAMATION AND CONSERVATION

The first message of President Roosevelt to Congress contained these words: "The forest and water problems are perhaps the most vital internal questions of the United States." At that moment, on December 3, 1901, the impulse was given that was to add to the American vocabulary two new words, "reclamation" and "conservation," that was to create two great constructive movements for the preservation, the increase, and the utilization of natural resources, and that was to establish a new relationship on the part of the Federal Government to the nation's natural wealth.

Reclamation and conservation had this in common: the purpose of both was the intelligent and efficient utilization of the natural resources of the country for the benefit of the people of the country. But they differed in one respect, and with conspicuous practical effects. Reclamation, which meant the spending of public moneys to render fertile and usable arid lands hitherto deemed worthless, trod on no one's toes. It took from no one anything that he had; it interfered with no one's enjoyment of benefits which it was not in the public interest that he should continue to enjoy unchecked. It was therefore popular from the first, and the new policy went through Congress as though on well-oiled wheels. Only six months passed between its first statement in the Presidential message and its enactment into law. Conservation, on the other hand, had to begin by withholding the natural resources from exploitation and extravagant use. It had, first of all, to establish in the national mind the principle that the forests and mines of the nation are not an inexhaustible grab-bag into which whosoever will may thrust greedy and wasteful hands, and by this new understanding to stop the squandering of vast national resources until they could be economically developed and intelligently used. So it was inevitable that conservation should prove unpopular, while reclamation gained an easy popularity, and that those who had been feeding fat off the country's stores of forest and mineral wealth should oppose, with tooth and nail, the very suggestion of conservation. It was on the first Sunday after he reached Washington as President, before he had moved into the White House, that Roosevelt discussed with two men, Gifford Pinchot and F. H. Newell, the twin policies that were to become two of the finest contributions to American progress of the Roosevelt Administrations. Both men were already in the Government service, both were men of broad vision and high constructive ability; with both Roosevelt had already worked when he was Governor of New York. The name of Newell, who became chief engineer of the Reclamation Service, ought to be better known popularly than it is in connection with the wonderful work that has been accomplished in making the desert lands of western America blossom and produce abundantly. The name of Pinchot, by a more fortunate combination of events, has become synonymous in the popular mind with the conservation movement.

On the very day that the first Roosevelt message was read to the Congress, a committee of Western Senators and Congressmen was organized, under the leadership of Senator Francis G. Newlands of Nevada, to prepare a Reclamation Bill. The only obstacle to the prompt enactment of the bill was the undue insistence upon State Rights by certain Congressmen, "who consistently fought for local and private interests as against the interests of the people as a whole." In spite of this shortsighted opposition, the bill became law on June 17, 1902, and the work of reclamation began without an instant's delay. The Reclamation Act set aside the proceeds of the sale of public lands for the purpose of reclaiming the waste areas of the arid West.

Lands otherwise worthless were to be irrigated and in those new regions of agricultural productivity homes were to be established. The money so expended was to be repaid in due course by the settlers on the land and the sums repaid were to be used as a revolving fund for the continuous prosecution of the reclamation work. Nearly five million dollars was made immediately available for the work. Within four years, twenty-six "projects" had been approved by the Secretary of the Interior and work was well under way on practically all of them. They were situated in fourteen States--Arizona, Colorado, Idaho, Kansas, Montana, Nebraska, Washington, Utah, Wyoming, New Mexico, North Dakota, Oregon, California,

South Dakota. The individual projects were intended to irrigate areas of from eight thousand to two hundred thousand acres each; and the grand total of arid lands to which water was thus to be brought by canals, tunnels, aqueducts, and ditches was more than a million and a half acres.

The work had to be carried out under the most difficult and adventurous conditions. The men of the Reclamation Service were in the truest sense pioneers, building great engineering works far from the railroads, where the very problem of living for the great numbers of workers required was no simple one. On the Shoshone in Wyoming these men built the highest dam in the world, 310 feet from base to crest. They pierced a mountain range in Colorado and carried the waters of the Gunnison River nearly six miles to the Uncompahgre Valley through a tunnel in the solid rock. The great Roosevelt dam on the Salt River in Arizona with its gigantic curved wall of masonry 280 feet high, created a lake with a capacity of fifty-six billion cubic feet, and watered in 1915 an area of 750,000 acres.

The work of these bold pioneers was made possible by the fearless backing which they received from the Administration at Washington. The President demanded of them certain definite results and gave them unquestioning support. In Roosevelt's own words, "the men in charge were given to understand that they must get into the water if they would learn to swim; and, furthermore, they learned to know that if they acted honestly, and boldly and fearlessly accepted responsibility, I would stand by them to the limit. In this, as in every other case, in the end the boldness of the action fully justified itself."

The work of reclamation was first prosecuted under the United States Geological Survey; but in the spring of 1908 the United States Reclamation Service was established to carry it on, under the direction of Mr. Newell, to whom the inception of the plan was due. Roosevelt paid a fine and well-deserved tribute to the man who originated and carried through this great national achievement when he said that "Newell's single-minded devotion to this great task, the constructive imagination which enabled him to conceive it, and the executive power and high character through which he and his assistant, Arthur P. Davis, built up a model service--all these made him a model servant. The final proof of his merit is supplied by the character and records of the men who later assailed him."

The assault to which Roosevelt thus refers was the inevitable aftermath of great accomplishment. Reclamation was popular, when it was proposed, while it was being carried out, and when the water began to flow in the ditches, making new lands of fertile abundance for settlers and farmers. But the reaction of unpopularity came the minute the beneficiaries had to begin to pay for the benefits received. Then arose a concerted movement for the repudiation of the obligation of the settlers to repay the Government for what had been spent to reclaim the land. The baser part of human nature always seeks a scapegoat; and it might naturally be expected that the repudiators and their supporters should concentrate their attacks upon the head of the Reclamation Service, to whose outstanding ability and continuous labor they owed that for which they were now unwilling to pay. But no attack, not even the adverse report of an ill-humored congressional committee, can alter the fact of the tremendous service that Newell and his loyal associates in the Reclamation Service did for the nation and the people of the United States. By 1915 reclamation had added to the arable land of the country a million and a quarter acres, of which nearly eight hundred thousand acres were already "under water," and largely under tillage, producing yearly more than eighteen million dollars' worth of crops.

When Roosevelt became President there was a Bureau of Forestry in the Department of Agriculture, but it was a body entrusted with merely the study of forestry problems and principles. It contained all the trained foresters in the employ of the Government; but it had no public forest lands whatever to which the knowledge and skill of these men could be applied. All the forest reserves of that day were in the charge of the Public Land Office in the Department of the Interior. This was managed by clerks who knew nothing of forestry, and most, if not all, of whom had never seen a stick of the timber or an acre of the woodlands for which they were responsible. The mapping and description of the timber lay with the Geological Survey. So the national forests had no foresters and the Government foresters no forests.

It was a characteristic arrangement of the old days. More than that, it was a characteristic expression of the old attitude of thought and action on the part of the American people toward their natural resources. Dazzled and intoxicated by the inexhaustible riches of their bountiful land, they had concerned themselves only with the agreeable task of utilizing and consuming them. To their shortsighted vision there seemed always plenty more beyond. With the beginning of the twentieth century a prophet arose in the land to warn the people that the supply was not inexhaustible. He declared not only that the "plenty more beyond" had an end, but that the end was already in sight. This prophet was Gifford Pinchot. His warning went forth reinforced by all the authority of the Presidential office and all the conviction and driving power of the personality of Roosevelt himself. Pinchot's warning cry was startling:

"The growth of our forests is but one-third of the annual cut; and we have in store timber enough for only twenty or thirty years at our present rate of use.... Our coal supplies are so far from being inexhaustible that if the increasing rate of consumption shown by the figures of the last seventy-five years continues to prevail, our supplies of anthracite coal will last but fifty years and of bituminous coal less than two hundred years.... Many oil and gas fields, as in Pennsylvania, West Virginia, and the Mississippi Valley, have already failed, yet vast quantities of gas continue to be poured into the air and great quantities of oil into the streams. Cases are known in which great volumes of oil were systematically burned in order to get rid of it.... In 1896, Professor Shaler, than whom no one has spoken with greater authority on this subject, estimated that in the upland regions of the States South of Pennsylvania, three thousand square miles of soil have been destroyed as the result of forest denudation, and that destruction was then proceeding at the rate of one hundred square miles of fertile soil per year.. ... The Mississippi River alone is estimated to transport yearly four hundred million tons of sediment, or about twice the amount of material to be excavated from the Panama Canal. This material is the most fertile portion of the richest fields, transformed from a blessing to a curse by unrestricted erosion.... The destruction of forage plants by overgrazing has resulted, in the opinion of men most capable of judging, in reducing the grazing value of the public lands by one-half."

Here, then, was a problem of national significance, and it was one which the President attacked with his usual promptness and vigor. His first message to Congress called for the unification of the care of the forest lands of the public domain in a single body under the Department of Agriculture. He asked that legal authority be granted to the President to transfer to the Department of Agriculture lands for use as forest reserves. He declared that "the forest reserves should be set apart forever for the use and benefit of our people as a whole and not sacrificed to the shortsighted greed of a few." He supplemented this declaration with an explanation of the meaning and purpose of the forest policy which he urged should be adopted: "Wise forest protection does not mean the withdrawal of forest resources, whether of wood, water, or grass, from contributing their full share to the welfare of the people, but, on the contrary, gives the assurance of larger and more certain supplies. The fundamental idea of forestry is the perpetuation of forests by use. Forest protection is not an end in itself; it is a means to increase and sustain the resources of our country and the industries which depend upon them. The preservation of our forests is an imperative business necessity. We have come to see clearly that whatever destroys the forest, except to make way for agriculture, threatens our wellbeing."

Nevertheless it was four years before Congress could be brought to the common-sense policy of administering the forest lands still belonging to the Government. Pinchot and his associates in the Bureau of Forestry spent the interval profitably, however, in investigating and studying the whole problem of national forest resources and in drawing up enlightened and effective plans for their protection and development. Accordingly, when the act transferring the National Forests to the charge of the newly created United States Forest Service in the Department of Agriculture was passed early in 1905, they were ready for the responsibility.

The principles which they had formulated and which they now began to apply had been summed up by Roosevelt in the statement "that the rights of the public to the natural resources outweigh private rights and must be given the first consideration." Until the establishment of the Forest Service, private rights had almost always been allowed to overbalance public rights in matters that concerned not only the National Forests, but the public lands generally. It was the necessity of having this new principle recognized and adopted that made the way of the newly created Forest Service and of the whole Conservation movement so thorny. Those who had been used to making personal profit from free and unrestricted exploitation of the nation's natural resources would look only with antagonism on a movement which put a consideration of the general welfare first.

The Forest Service nevertheless put these principles immediately into practical application. The National Forests were opened to a regulated use of all their resources. A law was passed throwing open to settlement all land in the National Forests which was found to be chiefly valuable for agriculture. Hitherto all such land had been closed to the settler. Regulations were established and enforced which favored the settler rather than the large stockowner. It was provided that, when conditions required the reduction in the number of head of stock grazed in any National Forest, the vast herds of the wealthy owner should be affected before the few head of the small man, upon which the living of his family depended. The principle which excited the bitterest antagonism of all was the rule that any one, except a bona fide settler on the land, who took public property for private profit should pay for what he got. This was a new and most unpalatable idea to the big stock and sheep raisers, who had been accustomed to graze their animals at will on the richest lands of the public forests, with no one but themselves a penny the better off thereby. But the Attorney-General of the United States declared it legal to make the men who pastured their cattle and sheep in the National Forests pay for this privilege; and in the summer of 1906 such charges were for the first time made and collected. The trained foresters of the service were put in charge of the National Forests. As a result, improvement began to manifest itself in other ways. Within two years the fire prevention work alone had completely justified the new policy of forest regulation. Eighty-six per cent of the fires that did occur in the National Forests were held down to an area of five acres or less. The new service not only made rapid progress in saving the timber, but it began to make money for the nation by selling the timber. In 1905 the sales of timber brought in $60,000; three years later the return was $850,000.

The National Forests were trebled in size during the two Roosevelt Administrations with the result that there were 194,000,000 acres of publicly owned and administered forest lands when Roosevelt went out of office. The inclusion of these lands in the National Forests, where they were safe from the selfish exploitation of greedy private interests, was not accomplished without the bitterest opposition. The wisdom of the serpent sometimes had to be called into play to circumvent the adroit maneuvering of these interests and their servants in Congress. In 1907, for example, Senator Charles W. Fulton of Oregon obtained an amendment to the Agricultural Appropriation Bill forbidding the President to set aside any additional National Forests in six Northwestern States.. But the President and the Forest Service were ready for this bold attempt to deprive the public of some 16,000,000 acres for the benefit of land grabbers and special interests. They knew exactly what lands ought to be set aside in those States. So the President first unostentatiously signed the necessary proclamations to erect those lands into National Forests, and then quietly approved the Agricultural Bill. "The opponents of the Forest Service," said Roosevelt, "turned handsprings in their wrath; and dire were their threats against the Executive; but the threats could not be carried out, and were really only a tribute to the efficiency of our action."

The development of a sound and enlightened forest policy naturally led to the consideration of a similar policy for dealing with the water power of the country which had hitherto gone to waste or was in the hands of private interests. It had been the immemorial custom that the water powers on the navigable streams, on the public domain, and in the National Forests should be given away for nothing, and practically without question, to the first comer. This ancient custom ran right athwart the newly enunciated principle that public property should not pass into private possession without being paid for, and that permanent grants, except for home-making, should not be made. The Forest Service now began to apply this principle to the water powers in the National Forests, granting permission for the development and use of such power for limited periods only and requiring payment for the privilege. This was the beginning of a general water power policy which, in the course of time, commended itself to public approval; but it was long before it ceased to be opposed by the private interests that wanted these rich resources for their own undisputed use.

Out of the forest movement grew the conservation movement in its broader sense. In the fall of 1907 Roosevelt made a trip down the Mississippi River with the definite purpose of drawing general attention to the subject of the development of the national inland waterways. Seven months before, he had established the Inland Waterways Commission and had directed it to "consider the relations of the streams to the use of all the great permanent natural resources and their conservation for the making and maintenance of permanent homes." During the trip a letter was prepared by a group of men interested in the conservation movement and was presented to him, asking him to summon a conference on the conservation of natural resources. At a great meeting held at Memphis, Tennessee, Roosevelt publicly announced his intention of calling such a conference.

In May of the following year the conference was held in the East Room of the

White House. There were assembled there the President, the Vice-President, seven Cabinet members, the Supreme Court Justices, the Governors of thirty-four States and representatives of the other twelve, the Governors of all the Territories, including Alaska, Hawaii, and Porto Rico, the President of the Board of Commissioners of the District of Columbia, representatives of sixty-eight national societies, four special guests, William Jennings Bryan, James J. Hill, Andrew Carnegie, and John Mitchell, forty-eight general guests, and the members of the Inland Waterways Commission. The object of the conference was stated by the President in these words: "It seems to me time for the country to take account of its natural resources, and to inquire how long they are likely to last. We are prosperous now; we should not forget that it will be just as important to our descendants to be prosperous in their time."

At the conclusion of the conference a declaration prepared by the Governors of Louisiana, New Jersey, Wisconsin, Utah, and South Carolina, was unanimously adopted. This Magna Charta of the conservation movement declared "that the great natural resources supply the material basis upon which our civilization must continue to depend and upon which the perpetuity of the nation itself rests," that "this material basis is threatened with exhaustion," and that "this conservation of our natural resources is a subject of transcendent importance, which should engage unremittingly the attention of the Nation, the States, and the people in earnest cooperation." It set forth the practical implications of Conservation in these words:

"We agree that the land should be so used that erosion and soil wash shall cease; and that there should be reclamation of arid and semi-arid regions by means of irrigation, and of swamp and overflowed regions by means of drainage; that the waters should be so conserved and used as to promote navigation, to enable the arid regions to be reclaimed by irrigation, and to develop power in the interests of the people; that the forests which regulate our rivers, support our industries, and promote the fertility and productiveness of the soil should be preserved and perpetuated; that the minerals found so abundantly beneath the surface should be so used as to prolong their utility; that the beauty, healthfulness, and habitability of our country should be preserved and increased; that sources of national wealth exist for the benefit of the people, and that monopoly thereof should not be tolerated."

The conference urged the continuation and extension of the forest policies already established; the immediate adoption of a wise, active, and thorough waterway policy for the prompt improvement of the streams, and the conservation of water resources for irrigation, water supply, power, and navigation; and the enactment of laws for the prevention of waste in the mining and extraction of coal, oil, gas, and other minerals with a view to their wise conservation for the use of the people. The declaration closed with the timely adjuration, "Let us conserve the foundations of our prosperity."

As a result of the conference President Roosevelt created the National Conservation Commission, consisting of forty-nine men of prominence, about one-third of whom were engaged in politics, one-third in various industries, and one-third in scientific work. Gifford Pinchot was appointed chairman. The Commission proceeded to make an inventory of the natural resources of the United States. This inventory contains the only authentic statement as to the amounts of the national resources of the country, the degree to which they have already been exhausted, and their probable duration. But with this inventory there came to an end the activity of the Conservation Commission, for Congress not only refused any appropriation for its use but decreed by law that no bureau of the Government should do any work for any commission or similar body appointed by the President, without reference to the question whether such work was appropriate or not for such a bureau to undertake. Inasmuch as the invaluable inventory already made had been almost entirely the work of scientific bureaus of the Government instructed by the President to cooperate with the Commission, the purpose and animus of this legislation were easily apparent. Congress had once more shown its friendship for the special interests and its indifference to the general welfare.

In February, 1909, on the invitation of President Roosevelt, a North American Conservation Conference, attended by representatives of the United States, Canada, and Mexico, was held at the White House. A declaration of principles was drawn up and the suggestion made that all the nations of the world should be invited to meet in a World Conservation Conference. The President forthwith addressed to forty-five nations a letter inviting them to assemble at The Hague for such a conference; but, as he has laconically expressed it, "When I left the White House the project lapsed."

# CHAPTER X. BEING WISE IN TIME

Perhaps the most famous of Roosevelt's epigrammatic sayings is, "Speak softly and carry a big stick." The public, with its instinctive preference for the dramatic over the significant, promptly seized upon the "big stick" half of the aphorism and ignored the other half. But a study of the various acts of Roosevelt when he was President readily shows that in his mind the "big stick" was purely subordinate. It was merely the ultima ratio, the possession of which would enable a nation to "speak softly" and walk safely along the road of peace and justice and fair play.

The secret of Roosevelt's success in foreign affairs is to be found in another of his favorite sayings: "Nine-tenths of wisdom is to be wise in time." He has himself declared that his whole foreign policy "was based on the exercise of intelligent foresight and of decisive action sufficiently far in advance of any likely crisis to make it improbable that we would run into serious trouble."

When Roosevelt became President, a perplexing controversy with Great Britain over the boundary line between Alaska and Canada was in full swing. The problem, which had become acute with the discovery of gold in the Klondike in 1897, had already been considered, together with eleven other subjects of dispute between Canada and the United States, by a Joint Commission which had been able to reach no agreement. The essence of the controversy was this: The treaty of 1825 between Great Britain and Russia had declared that the boundary, dividing British and Russian America on that five-hundred-mile strip of land which depends from the Alaskan elephant's head like a dangling halter rope, should be drawn "parallel to the windings of the coast" at a distance inland of thirty miles. The United States took the plain and literal interpretation of these words in the treaty. The Canadian contention was that within the meaning of the treaty the fiords or inlets which here break into the land were not part of the sea, and that the line, instead of following, at the correct distance inland, the indentations made by these arms of the sea, should leap boldly across them, at the agreed distance from the points of the headlands. This would give Canada the heads of several great inlets and direct access to the sea far north of the point where the Canadian coast had, always been assumed to end. Canada and the United States were equally resolute in upholding their claims. It looked as if the matter would end in a deadlock.

John Hay, who had been Secretary of State in McKinley's Cabinet, as he now was in Roosevelt's, had done his best to bring the matter to a settlement, but had been unwilling to have the dispute arbitrated, for the very good reason that, as he said, "although our claim is as clear as the sun in heaven, we know enough of arbitration to foresee the fatal tendency of all arbitrators to compromise." Roosevelt believed that the "claim of the Canadians for access to deep water along any part of the Alaskan coast is just exactly as indefensible as if they should now claim the island of Nantucket." He was willing, however, to refer the question unconfused by other issues to a second Joint Commission of six. The commission was duly constituted. There was no odd neutral member of this body, as in an arbitration, but merely three representatives from each side. Of the British representatives two were Canadians and the third was the Lord Chief Justice of England, Lord Alverstone.

But before the Commission met, the President took pains to have conveyed to the British Cabinet, in an informal but diplomatically correct way, his views and his intentions in the event of a disagreement. "I wish to make one last effort," he said, "to bring about an agreement through the Commission which will enable the people of both countries to say that the result represents the feeling of the representatives of both countries. But if there is a disagreement, I wish it distinctly understood, not only that there will be no arbitration of the matter, but that in my message to Congress I shall take a position which will prevent any possibility of arbitration hereafter." If this should seem to any one too vigorous flourishing of the "big stick," let him remember that it was all done through confidential diplomatic channels, and that the judgment of the Lord Chief Justice of England, when the final decision was made, fully upheld Roosevelt's position.

The decision of the Commission was, with slight immaterial modifications, in favor of the United States. Lord Alverstone voted against his Canadian than colleagues. It was a just decision, as most well-informed Canadians knew at the time. The troublesome question was settled; the time-honored friendship of two great peoples had suffered no interruption; and Roosevelt had secured for his country its just due, without public parade or bluster, by merely being wise--and inflexible--in time.

During the same early period of his Presidency, Roosevelt found himself confronted with a situation in South America, which threatened a serious violation of the Monroe Doctrine. Venezuela was repudiating certain debts which the Venezuelan Government had guaranteed to European capitalists. German capital was chiefly involved, and Germany proposed to collect the debts by force. Great Britain and Italy were also concerned in the matter, but Germany was the ringleader and the active partner in the undertaking. Throughout the year 1902 a pacific blockade of the Venezuelan coast was maintained and in December of that year an ultimatum demanding the immediate payment of the debts was presented. When its terms were not complied with, diplomatic relations were broken off and the Venezuelan fleet was seized. At this point the United States entered upon the scene, but with no blare of trumpets.

In fact, what really happened was not generally known until several years later.

In his message of December, 1901, President Roosevelt had made two significant statements. Speaking of the Monroe Doctrine, he said, "We do not guarantee any state against punishment, if it misconducts itself." This was very satisfactory to Germany. But he added--"provided the punishment does not take the form of the acquisition of territory by any non-American power." This did not suit the German book so well. For a year the matter was discussed. Germany disclaimed any intention to make "permanent" acquisitions in Venezuela but contended for its right to make "temporary" ones. Now the world had already seen "temporary" acquisitions made in China, and it was a matter of common knowledge that this convenient word was often to be interpreted in a Pickwickian sense.

When the "pacific blockade" passed into the stage of active hostilities, the patience of Roosevelt snapped. The German Ambassador, von Holleben, was summoned to the White House. The President proposed to him that Germany should arbitrate its differences with Venezuela. Von Holleben assured him that his "Imperial Master" would not hear of such a course. The President persisted that there must be no taking possession, even temporarily, of Venezuelan territory. He informed the Ambassador that Admiral Dewey was at that moment maneuvering in Caribbean waters, and that if satisfactory assurances did not come from Berlin in ten days, he would be ordered to proceed to Venezuela to see that no territory was seized by German forces. The Ambassador was firm in his conviction that no assurances would be forthcoming.

A week later Von Holleben appeared at the White House to talk of another matter and was about to leave without mentioning Venezuela. The President stopped him with a question. No, said the Ambassador, no word had come from Berlin. Then, Roosevelt explained, it would not be necessary for him to wait the remaining three days. Dewey would be instructed to sail a day earlier than originally planned. He added that not a word of all this had been put upon paper, and that if the German Emperor would consent to arbitrate, the President would praise him publicly for his broadmindedness. The Ambassador was still convinced that no arbitration was conceivable.

But just twelve hours later he appeared at the White House, his face wreathed in smiles. On behalf of his Imperial Master he had the honor to request the President of the United States to act as arbitrator between Germany and Venezuela. The orders to Dewey were never sent, the President publicly congratulated the Kaiser on his loyalty to the principle of arbitration, and, at Roosevelt's suggestion, the case went to The Hague. Not an intimation of the real occurrences came out till long after, not a public word or act marred the perfect friendliness of the two nations. The Monroe Doctrine was just as unequivocally invoked and just as inflexibly upheld as it had been by Grover Cleveland eight years before in another Venezuelan case. But the quiet private warning had been substituted for the loud public threat.

The question of the admission of Japanese immigrants to the United States and of their treatment had long disturbed American international relations. It became acute in the latter part of 1906, when the city of San Francisco determined to exclude all Japanese pupils from the public schools and to segregate them in a school of their own. This action seemed to the Japanese a manifest violation of the rights guaranteed by treaty. Diplomatic protests were instantly forthcoming at Washington; and popular demonstrations against the United States boiled up in Tokyo. For the third time there appeared splendid material for a serious conflict with a great power which might conceivably lead to active hostilities. From such beginnings wars have come before now.

The President was convinced that the Californians were utterly wrong in what they had done, but perfectly right in the underlying conviction from which their action sprang. He saw that justice and good faith demanded that the Japanese in California be protected in their treaty rights, and that the Californians be protected from the immigration of Japanese laborers in mass. With characteristic promptness and vigor he set forth these two considerations and took action to make them effective. In his message to Congress in December he declared: "In the matter now before me, affecting the Japanese, everything that is in my power to do will be done and all of the forces, military and civil, of the United States which I may lawfully employ will be so employed ... to enforce the rights of aliens under treaties." Here was reassurance for the Japanese. But he also added: "The Japanese would themselves not tolerate the intrusion into their country of a mass of Americans who would displace Japanese in the business of the land. The people of California are right in insisting that the Japanese shall not come thither in mass." Here was reassurance for the Californians.

The words were promptly followed by acts. The garrison of Federal troops at San Francisco was reinforced and public notice was given that violence against Japanese would be put down. Suits were brought both in the California State courts and in the Federal courts there to uphold the treaty rights of Japan. Mr. Victor H. Metcalf, the Secretary of Commerce and Labor, himself a Californian, was sent to San Francisco to make a study of the whole situation. It was made abundantly clear to the people of San Francisco and the Coast that the provision of the Federal Constitution making treaties a part of the supreme law of the land, with which the Constitution and laws of no State can interfere, would be strictly enforced. The report of Secretary Metcalf showed that the school authorities of San Francisco had done not only an illegal thing but an unnecessary and a stupid thing.

Meanwhile Roosevelt had been working with equal vigor upon the other side of the problem. He esteemed it precisely as important to protect the Californians from the Japanese as to protect the Japanese from the Californians. As in the Alaskan and Venezuelan cases, he proceeded without beat of drum or clash of cymbal.

The matter was worked out in unobtrusive conferences between the President and the State Department and the Japanese representatives in Washington. It was all friendly, informal, conciliatory--but the Japanese did not fail to recognize the inflexible determination behind this courteous friendliness. Out of these conferences came an informal agreement on the part of the Japanese Government that no passports would be issued to Japanese workingmen permitting them to leave Japan for ports of the United States. It was further only necessary to prevent Japanese coolies from coming into the United States through Canada and Mexico. This was done by executive order just two days after the school authorities of San Francisco had rescinded their discriminatory school decree.

The incident is eminently typical of Roosevelt's principles and practice: to accord full measure of justice while demanding full measure in return; to be content with the fact without care for the formality; to see quickly, to look far, and to act boldly.

It had a sequel which rounded out the story. The President's ready willingness to compel California to do justice to the Japanese was misinterpreted in Japan as timidity. Certain chauvinistic elements in Japan began to have thoughts which were in danger of becoming inimical to the best interests of the United States. It seemed to President Roosevelt an opportune moment, for many reasons, to send the American battle fleet on a voyage around the world. The project was frowned on in this country and viewed with doubt in other parts of the world. Many said the thing could not be done, for no navy in the world had yet done it; but Roosevelt knew that it could. European observers believed that it would lead to war with Japan; but Roosevelt's conviction was precisely the opposite. In his own words, "I did not expect it;... I believed that Japan would feel as friendly in the matter as we did; but... if my expectations had proved mistaken, it would have been proof positive that we were going to be attacked anyhow, and... in such event it would have been an enormous gain to have had the three months' preliminary preparation which enabled the fleet to start perfectly equipped. In a personal interview before they left, I had explained to the officers in command that I believed the trip would be one of absolute peace, but that they were to take exactly the same precautions against sudden attack of any kind as if we were at war with all the nations of the earth; and that no excuse of any kind would be accepted if there were a sudden attack of any kind and we were taken unawares." Prominent inhabitants and newspapers of the Atlantic coast were deeply concerned over the taking away of the fleet from the Atlantic to the Pacific. The head of the Senate Committee on Naval Affairs, who hailed from the State of Maine, declared that the fleet should not and could not go because Congress would refuse to appropriate the money; Roosevelt announced in response that he had enough money to take the fleet around into the Pacific anyhow, that it would certainly go, and that if Congress did not choose to appropriate enough money to bring the fleet back, it could stay there. There was no further difficulty about the money.

The voyage was at once a hard training trip and a triumphant progress. Everywhere the ships, their officers, and their men were received with hearty cordiality and deep admiration, and nowhere more so than in Japan. The nations of the world were profoundly impressed by the achievement. The people of the United States were thoroughly aroused to a new pride in their navy and an interest in its adequacy and efficiency. It was definitely established in the minds of Americans and foreigners that the United States navy is rightfully as much at home in the Pacific as in the Atlantic. Any cloud the size of a man's hand that may have been gathering above the Japanese horizon was forthwith swept away. Roosevelt's plan was a novel and bold use of the instruments of war on behalf of peace which was positively justified in the event.

# CHAPTER XI. RIGHTS, DUTIES, AND REVOLUTIONS

It was a favorite conviction of Theodore Roosevelt that neither an individual nor a nation can possess rights which do not carry with them duties. Not long after the Venezuelan incident--in which the right of the United States, as set forth in the Monroe Doctrine, to prevent European powers from occupying territory in the Western Hemisphere was successfully upheld--an occasion arose nearer home not only to insist upon rights but to assume the duties involved. In a message to the Senate in February, 1905, Roosevelt thus outlined his conception of the dual nature of the Monroe Doctrine:

"It has for some time been obvious that those who profit by the Monroe Doctrine must accept certain responsibilities along with the rights which it confers, and that the same statement applies to those who uphold the doctrine.... An aggrieved nation can, without interfering with the Monroe Doctrine, take what action it sees fit in the adjustment of its disputes with American states, provided that action does not take the shape of interference with their form of government or of the despoilment of their territory under any disguise. But short of this, when the question is one of a money claim, the only way which remains finally to collect it is a blockade or bombardment or seizure of the custom houses, and this means... what is in effect a possession, even though only a temporary possession, of territory. The United States then becomes a party in interest, because under the Monroe Doctrine it cannot see any European power seize and permanently occupy the territory of one of these republics; and yet such seizure of territory, disguised or undisguised, may eventually offer the only way in which the power in question can collect its debts, unless there is interference on the part of the United States."

Roosevelt had already found such interference necessary in the case of Germany and Venezuela. But it had been interference in a purely negative sense. He had merely insisted that the European power should not occupy American territory even temporarily. In the later case of the Dominican Republic he supplemented this negative interference with positive action based upon his conviction of the inseparable nature of rights and obligations.

Santo Domingo was in its usual state of chronic revolution. The stakes for which the rival forces were continually fighting were the custom houses, for they were the only certain sources of revenue and their receipts were the only reliable security which could be offered to foreign capitalists in support of loans. So thoroughgoing was the demoralization of the Republic's affairs that at one time there were two rival "governments" in the island and a revolution going on against each. One of these governments was once to be found at sea in a small gunboat but still insisting that, as the only legitimate government, it was entitled to declare war or peace or, more particularly, to make loans. The national debt of the Republic had mounted to $32,280,000 of which some $22,000,000 was owed to European creditors. The interest due on it in the year 1905 was two and a half million dollars. The whole situation was ripe for intervention by one or more European governments.

Such action President Roosevelt could not permit. But he could not ignore the validity of the debts which the Republic had contracted or the justice of the demand for the payment of at least the interest. "It cannot in the long run prove possible," he said, "for the United States to protect delinquent American nations from punishment for the non-performance of their duties unless she undertakes to make them perform their duties." So he invented a plan, which, by reason of its success in the Dominican case and its subsequent application and extension by later administrations, has come to be a thoroughly accepted part of the foreign policy of the United States. It ought to be known as the Roosevelt Plan, just as the amplification of the Monroe Doctrine already outlined might well be known as the Roosevelt Doctrine.

A naval commander in Dominican waters was instructed to see that no revolutionary fighting was permitted to endanger the custom houses. These instructions were carried out explicitly but without any actual use of force or shedding of blood. On one occasion two rival forces had planned a battle in a custom-house town. The American commander informed them courteously but firmly that they would not be permitted to fight there, for a battle might endanger the custom house. He had no objection, however, to their fighting. In fact he had picked out a nice spot for them outside the town where they might have their battle undisturbed. The winner could have the town. Would they kindly step outside for their fight. They would; they did. The American commander gravely welcomed the victorious faction as the rightful rulers of the town. So much for keeping the custom houses intact. But the Roosevelt Plan went much further. An agreement was entered into with those governmental authorities "who for the moment seemed best able to speak for the country" by means of which the custom houses were placed under American control. United States forces were to keep order and to protect the custom houses; United States officials were to collect the customs dues; forty-five per cent of the revenue was to be turned over to the Dominican Government, and fifty-five per cent put into a sinking fund in New York for the benefit of the creditors. The plan succeeded famously. The Dominicans got more out of their forty-five per cent than they had been wont to get when presumably the entire revenue was theirs. The creditors thoroughly approved, and their Governments had no possible pretext left for interference. Although the plan concerned itself not at all with the internal affairs of the Republic, its indirect influence was strong for good and the island enjoyed a degree of peace and prosperity such as it had not known before for at least a century. There was, however, strong opposition in the United States Senate to the ratification of the treaty with the Dominican Republic. The Democrats, with one or two exceptions, voted against ratification. A number of the more reactionary Republican Senators, also, who were violently hostile to President Roosevelt because of his attitude toward great corporations, lent their opposition. The Roosevelt Plan was further attacked by certain sections of the press, already antagonistic on other grounds, and by some of those whom Roosevelt called the "professional interventional philanthropists." It was two years before the Senate was ready to ratify the treaty, but meanwhile Roosevelt continued to carry it out "as a simple agreement on the part of the Executive which could be converted into a treaty whenever the Senate was ready to act."

The treaty as finally ratified differed in some particulars from the protocol. In the protocol the United States agreed "to respect the complete territorial integrity of the Dominican Republic." This covenant was omitted in the final document in deference to Roosevelt's opponents who could see no difference between "respecting" the integrity of territory and "guaranteeing" it. Another clause pledging the assistance of the United States in the internal affairs of the Republic, whenever the judgment of the American Government deemed it to be wise, was also omitted. The provision of the protocol making it the duty of the United States to deal with the various creditors of the Dominican Republic in order to determine the amount which each was to receive in settlement of its claims was modified so that this responsibility remained with the Government of the Republic. In Roosevelt's opinion, these modifications in the protocol detracted nothing from the original plan. He ascribed the delay in the ratification of the treaty to partisanship and bitterness against himself; and it is certainly true that most of the treaty's opponents were his consistent critics on other grounds.

A considerable portion of Roosevelt's success as a diplomat was the fruit of personality, as must be the case with any diplomat who makes more than a routine achievement. He disarmed suspicion by transparent honesty, and he impelled respect for his words by always promising or giving warning of not a hairsbreadth more than he was perfectly willing and thoroughly prepared to perform. He was always cheerfully ready to let the other fellow "save his face." He set no store by public triumphs. He was as exigent that his country should do justly as he was insistent that it should be done justly by. Phrases had no lure for him, appearances no glamour.

It was inevitable that so commanding a personality should have an influence beyond the normal sphere of his official activities. Only a man who had earned the confidence and the respect of the statesmen of other nations could have performed such a service as he did in 1905 in bringing about peace between Russia and Japan in the conflict then raging in the Far East. It was high time that the war should end, in the interest of both contestants. The Russians had been consistently defeated on land and had lost their entire fleet at the battle of Tsushima. The Japanese were apparently on the highroad to victory. But in reality, Japan's success had been bought at an exorbitant price. Intelligent observers in the diplomatic world who were in a position to realize the truth knew that neither nation could afford to go on.

On June 8, 1905, President Roosevelt sent to both Governments an identical note in which he urged them, "not only for their own sakes, but in the interest of the whole civilized world, to open direct negotiations for peace with each other." This was the first that the world heard of the proposal. But the President had already conducted, with the utmost secrecy, confidential negotiations with Tokyo and with St. Petersburg to induce both belligerents to consent to a face to face discussion of peace. In Russia he had found it necessary to go directly to the Czar himself, through the American Ambassador, George von Lengerke Meyer. Each Government was assured that no breath of the matter would be made public until both nations had signified their willingness to treat. Neither nation was to know anything of the other's readiness until both had committed themselves. These advances appear to have been made following a suggestion from Japan that Roosevelt should attempt to secure peace. He used to say, in discussing the matter, that, while it was not generally known or even suspected, Japan was actually "bled white" by the herculean efforts she had made. But Japan's position was the stronger, and peace was more important for Russia than for her antagonist. The Japanese were more clear-sighted than the selfish Russian bureaucracy; and they realized that they had gained so much already that there was nothing to be won by further fighting.

When the public invitation to peace negotiations was extended, the conference had already been arranged and the confidential consent of both Governments needed only to be made formal. Russia wished the meeting of plenipotentiaries to take place at Paris, Japan preferred Chifu, in China. Neither liked the other's suggestion, and Roosevelt's invitation to come to Washington, with the privilege of adjourning to some place in New England if the weather was too hot, was finally accepted. The formal meeting between the plenipotentiaries took place at Oyster Bay on the 5th of August on board the Presidential yacht, the Mayflower. Roosevelt received his guests in the cabin and proposed a toast in these words: "Gentlemen, I propose a toast to which there will be no answer and which I ask you to drink in silence, standing. I drink to the welfare and prosperity of the sovereigns and the peoples of the two great nations whose representatives have met one another on this ship. It is my earnest hope and prayer, in the interest not only of these two great powers, but of all civilized mankind, that a just and lasting peace may speedily be concluded between them."

The two groups of plenipotentiaries were carried, each on an American naval vessel, to Portsmouth, New Hampshire, and there at the Navy Yard began their conference. Two-thirds of the terms proposed by Japan were promptly accepted by the Russian envoys. But an irretrievable split on the remainder seemed inevitable. Japan demanded a money indemnity and the cession of the southern half of the island of Saghalien, which Japanese forces had already occupied. These demands the Russians refused.

Then Roosevelt took a hand in the proceedings. He urged the Japanese delegates, through the Japanese Ambassador, to give up their demand for an indemnity. He pointed out that, when it came to "a question of rubles," the Russian Government and the Russian people were firmly resolved not to yield. To Baron Rosen, one of the Russian delegates, he recommended yielding in the matter of Saghalien, since the Japanese were already in possession and there were racial and historical grounds for considering the southern half of the island logically Japanese territory. The envoys met again, and the Japanese renewed their demands. The Russians refused. Then the Japanese offered to waive the indemnity if the Russians would yield on Saghalien. The offer was accepted, and the peace was made.

Immediately Roosevelt was acclaimed by the world, including the Russians and the Japanese, as a great peacemaker. The Nobel Peace Prize of a medal and $40,000 was awarded to him. But it was not long before both in Russia and Japan public opinion veered to the point of asserting that he had caused peace to be made too soon and to the detriment of the interests of the nation in question. That was just what he expected. He knew human nature thoroughly; and from long experience he had learned to be humorously philosophical about such manifestations of man's ingratitude.

In the next year the influence of Roosevelt's personality was again felt in affairs outside the traditional realm of American international interests. Germany was attempting to intrude in Morocco, where France by common consent had been the dominant foreign influence. The rattling of the Potsdam saber was threatening the tranquillity of the status quo. A conference of eleven European powers and the United States was held at Algeciras to readjust the treaty provisions for the protection of foreigners in the decadent Moroccan empire. In the words of a historian of America's foreign relations, "Although the United States was of all perhaps the least directly interested in the subject matter of dispute, and might appropriately have held aloof from the meeting altogether, its representatives were among the most influential of all, and it was largely owing to their sane and irenic influence that in the end a treaty was amicably made and signed."[7] But there was something behind all this. A quiet conference had taken place one day in the remote city of Washington. The President of the United States and the French Ambassador had discussed the approaching meeting at Algeciras. There was a single danger-point in the impending negotiations. The French must find a way around it. The Ambassador had come to the right man. He went out with a few words scratched on a card in the ragged Roosevelt handwriting containing a proposal for a solution.[8] The proposal went to Paris, then to Morocco. The solution was adopted by the conference, and the Hohenzollern menace to the peace of the world was averted for the moment. Once more Roosevelt had shown how being wise in time was the sure way to peace.

Roosevelt's most important single achievement as President of the United States was the building of the Panama Canal. The preliminary steps which he took in order to make its building possible have been, of all his executive acts, the most consistently and vigorously criticized.

It is not our purpose here to follow at length the history of American diplomatic relations with Colombia and Panama. We are primarily concerned with the part which Roosevelt played in certain international occurrences, of which the Panama incident was not the least interesting and significant. In after years Roosevelt said laconically, "I took Panama." In fact he did nothing of the sort. But it was like him to brush aside all technical defenses of any act of his and to meet his critics on their own ground. It was as though he said to them, "You roundly denounce me for what I did at the time of the revolution which established the Republic of Panama. You declare that my acts were contrary to international law and international morals. I have a splendid technical defense on the legal side; but I care little about technicalities when compared with reality. Let us admit that I did what you charge me with. I will prove to you that I was justified in so doing. I took Panama; but the taking was a righteous act."

Fourteen years after that event, in a speech which he made in Washington, Roosevelt expressed his dissatisfaction with the way in which President Wilson was conducting the Great War. He reverted to what he had done in relation to

---

7   Willie Fletcher Johnson, "America's Foreign Relations"
8   The author had this story direct from Mr. Roosevelt himself.

Panama and contrasted his action with the failure of the Wilson Administration to take prompt possession of two hundred locomotives which had been built in this country for the late Russian Government. This is what he said:

"What I think, of course, in my view of the proper governmental policy, should have been done was to take the two hundred locomotives and then discuss. That was the course that I followed, and to which I have ever since looked back with impenitent satisfaction, in reference to the Panama Canal. If you remember, Panama declared itself independent and wanted to complete the Panama Canal and opened negotiations with us. I had two courses open. I might have taken the matter under advisement and put it before the Senate, in which case we should have had a number of most able speeches on the subject. We would have had a number of very profound arguments, and they would have been going on now, and the Panama Canal would be in the dim future yet. We would have had half a century of discussion, and perhaps the Panama Canal. I preferred that we should have the Panama Canal first and the half century of discussion afterward. And now instead of discussing the canal before it was built, which would have been harmful, they merely discuss me--a discussion which I regard with benign interest."

The facts of the case are simple and in the main undisputed. Shortly after the inauguration of Roosevelt as President, a treaty was negotiated with Colombia for the building of a canal at Panama. It provided for the lease to the United States of a strip six miles wide across the Isthmus, and for the payment to Colombia of $10,000,000 down and $250,000 a year, beginning nine years later. The treaty was promptly ratified by the United States Senate. A special session of the Colombian Senate spent the summer marking time and adjourned after rejecting the treaty by a unanimous vote. The dominant motive for the rejection was greed. An attempt was first made by the dictatorial government that held the Colombian Congress in its mailed hand to extort a large payment from the French Canal Company, whose rights and property on the Isthmus were to be bought by the United States for $40,000,000. Then $15,000,000 instead of $10,000,000 was demanded from the United States. Finally an adroit and conscienceless scheme was invented by which the entire rights of the French Canal Company were to be stolen by the Colombian Government. This last plot, however, would involve a delay of a year or so. The treaty was therefore rejected in order to provide the necessary delay.

But the people of Panama wanted the Canal. They were tired of serving as the milch cow for the fattening of the Government at Bogota. So they quietly organized a revolution. It was a matter of common knowledge that it was coming. Roosevelt, as well as the rest of the world, knew it and, believing in the virtue of being wise in time, prepared for it. Several warships were dispatched to the Isthmus.

The revolution came off promptly as expected. It was bloodless, for the American naval forces, fulfilling the treaty obligations of the United States, prevented the Colombian troops on one side of the Isthmus from using the Panama Railroad to cross to the other side where the revolutionists were. So the revolutionists were undisturbed. A republic was immediately declared and immediately recognized by the United States. A treaty with the new Republic, which guaranteed its independence and secured the cession of a zone ten miles wide across the Isthmus, was drawn up inside of two weeks and ratified by both Senates within three months. Six weeks later an American commission was on the ground to plan the work of construction. The Canal was built. The "half century of discussion" which Roosevelt foresaw is now more than a third over, and the discussion shows no sign of lagging. But the Panama Canal is in use.

Was the President of the United States justified in preventing the Colombian Government from fighting on the Isthmus to put down the unanimous revolution of the people of Panama? That is precisely all that he did. He merely gave orders to the American admiral on the spot to "prevent the disembarkation of Colombian troops with hostile intent within the limits of the state of Panama." But that action was enough, for the Isthmus is separated from Colombia on the one hand by three hundred miles of sea, and on the other by leagues of pathless jungle.

Roosevelt himself has summed up the action of the United States in this way:

"From the beginning to the end our course was straightforward and in absolute accord with the highest of standards of international morality.... To have acted otherwise than I did would have been on my part betrayal of the interests of the United States, indifference to the interests of Panama, and recreancy to the interests of the world at large. Colombia had forfeited every claim to consideration; indeed, this is not stating the case strongly enough: she had so acted that yielding to her would have meant on our part that culpable form of weakness which stands on a level with wickedness.... We gave to the people of Panama, self-government, and freed them from subjection to alien oppressors. We did our best to get Colombia to let us treat her with more than generous justice; we exercised patience to beyond the verge of proper forbearance.... I deeply regretted, and now deeply regret, the fact that the Colombian Government rendered it imperative for me to take the action I took; but I had no alternative, consistent with the full performance of my duty to my own people, and to the nations of mankind."

The final verdict will be given only in another generation by the historian and by the world at large. But no portrait of Theodore Roosevelt, and no picture of his times, can be complete without the bold, firm outlines of his Panama policy set as near as may be in their proper perspective.

# CHAPTER XII. THE TAFT ADMINISTRATION

In the evening of that election day in 1904 which saw Roosevelt made President in his own right, after three years of the Presidency given him by fate, he issued a brief statement, in which he said: "The wise custom which limits the President to two terms regards the substance and not the form, and under no circumstances will I be a candidate for or accept another nomination." From this determination, which in his mind related to a third consecutive term, and to nothing else, he never wavered. Four years later, in spite of a widespread demand that he should be a candidate to succeed himself, he used the great influence and prestige of his position as President and leader of his party to bring about the nomination of his friend and close associate, William Howard Taft. The choice received general approval from the Republican party and from the country at large, although up to the very moment of the nomination in the convention at Chicago there was no certainty that a successful effort to stampede the convention for Roosevelt would not be made by his more irreconcilable supporters.

Taft was elected by a huge popular plurality. His opponent was William Jennings Bryan, who was then making his third unsuccessful campaign for the Presidency. Taft's election, like his nomination, was assured by the unreserved and dynamic support accorded him by President Roosevelt. Taft, of course, was already an experienced statesman, high in the esteem of the nation for his public record as Federal judge, as the first civil Governor of the Philippines, and as Secretary of War in the Roosevelt Cabinet. There was every reason to predict for him a successful and effective Administration. His occupancy of the White House began under smiling skies. He had behind him a united party and a satisfied public opinion. Even his political opponents conceded that the country would be safe in his hands. It was expected that he would be conservatively progressive and progressively conservative. Everybody believed in him. Yet within a year of the day of his inauguration the President's popularity was sharply on the wane. Two years after his election the voters repudiated the party which he led. By the end of his Presidential term the career which had begun with such happy auguries had become a political tragedy. There were then those who recalled the words of the Roman historian, "All would have believed him capable of governing if only he had not come to govern."

It was not that the Taft Administration was barren of achievement. On the contrary, its record of accomplishment was substantial. Of two amendments to the Federal Constitution proposed by Congress, one was ratified by the requisite number of States before Taft went out of office, and the other was finally ratified less than a month after the close of his term. These were the amendment authorizing the imposition of a Federal income tax and that providing for the direct election of United States Senators. Two States were admitted to the Union during Taft's term of office, New Mexico and Arizona, the last Territories of the United States on the continent, except Alaska.

Other achievements of importance during Taft's Administration were the establishment of the parcels post and the postal savings banks; the requirement of publicity, through sworn statements of the candidates, for campaign contributions for the election of Senators and Representatives; the extension of the authority of the Interstate Commerce Commission over telephone, telegraph, and cable lines; an act authorizing the President to withdraw public lands from entry for the purpose of conserving the natural resources which they may contain--something which Roosevelt had already done without specific statutory authorization; the establishment of a Commerce Court to hear appeals from decisions of the Interstate Commerce Commission; the appointment of a commission, headed by President Hadley of Yale, to investigate the subject of railway stock and bond issues, and to propose a law for the Federal supervision of such railway securities; the Mann "white slave" act, dealing with the transfer of women from one State to another for immoral purposes; the establishment of the Children's Bureau in the Department of Commerce and Labor; the empowering of the Interstate Commerce Commission to investigate all railway accidents; the creation of Forest Reserves in the White Mountains and in the southern Appalachians.

Taft's Administration was further marked, by economy in expenditure, by a considerable extension of the civil service law to cover positions in the executive departments hitherto free plunder for the spoilsmen, and by efforts on the part of the President to increase the efficiency and the economical administration of the public service.

But this good record of things achieved was not enough to gain for Mr. Taft popular approval. Items on the other side of the ledger were pointed out. Of these the three most conspicuous were the Payne-Aldrich tariff, the Ballinger-Pinchot controversy, and the insurgent movement in Congress.

The Republican party was returned to power in 1908, committed to a revision of the tariff. Though the party platform did not so state, this was generally interpreted as a pledge of revision downward. Taft made it clear during his campaign that such was his own reading of the party pledge. He said, for instance, "It is my judgment that there are many schedules of the tariff in which the rates are excessive, and there are a few in which the rates are not sufficient to fill the measure of conservative protection. It is my judgment that a revision of the tariff in accordance with the pledge of the platform, will be, on the whole, a substantial revision downward, though there probably will be a few exceptions in this regard." Five months after Taft's inauguration the Payne-Aldrich bill became law with his signature. In signing it the President said, "The bill is not a perfect bill or a complete compliance with the promises made, strictly interpreted"; but he further declared that he signed it because he believed it to be "the result of a sincere effort on the part of the Republican party to make downward revision."

This view was not shared by even all Republicans. Twenty of them in the House voted against the bill on its final passage, and seven of them in the Senate. They represented the Middle West and the new element and spirit in the Republican party. Their dissatisfaction with the performance of their party associates in Congress and in the White House was shared by their constituents and by many other Republicans throughout the country. A month after the signing of the tariff law, Taft made a speech at Winona, Minnesota, in support of Congressman James A. Tawney, the one Republican representative from Minnesota who had not voted against the bill. In the course of that speech he said; "This is the best tariff bill that the Republican party has ever passed, and, therefore, the best tariff bill that has been passed at all."

He justified Mr. Tawney's action in voting for the bill and his own in signing it on the ground that "the interests of the country, the interests of the party" required the sacrifice of the accomplishment of certain things in the revision of the tariff which had been hoped for, "in order to maintain party solidity," which he believed to be much more important than the reduction of rates in one or two schedules of the tariff.

A second disaster to the Taft Administration came in the famous Ballinger-Pinchot controversy. Louis R. Glavis, who had served as a special agent of the General Land Office to investigate alleged frauds in certain claims to coal lands in Alaska, accused Richard Ballinger, the Secretary of the Interior, of favoritism toward those who were attempting to get public lands fraudulently. The charges were vigorously supported by Mr. Pinchot, who broadened the accusation to cover a general indifference on the part of the Secretary of the Interior to the whole conservation movement. President Taft, however, completely exonerated Secretary Ballinger from blame and removed Glavis for "filing a disingenuous statement unjustly impeaching the official integrity of his superior officer." Later Pinchot was also dismissed from the service. The charges against Secretary Ballinger were investigated by a joint committee of Congress, a majority of which exonerated the accused Cabinet officer. Nevertheless the whole controversy, which raged with virulence for many months, convinced many ardent supporters of the conservation movement, and especially many admirers of Mr. Pinchot and of Roosevelt, that the Taft Administration at the best was possessed of little enthusiasm for conservation. There was a widespread belief, as well, that the President had handled the whole matter maladroitly and that in permitting himself to be driven to a point where he had to deprive the country of the services of Gifford Pinchot, the originator of the conservation movement, he had displayed unsound judgment and deplorable lack of administrative ability.

The first half of Mr. Taft's term was further marked by acute dissensions in the Republican ranks in Congress. Joseph G. Cannon was Speaker of the House, as he had been in three preceding Congresses. He was a reactionary Republican of the most pronounced type. Under his leadership the system of autocratic party control of legislation in the House had been developed to a high point of effectiveness. The Speaker's authority had become in practice almost unrestricted.

In the congressional session of 1909-10 a strong movement of insurgency arose within the Republican party in Congress against the control of the little band of leaders dominated by the Speaker. In March, 1910, the Republican Insurgents, forty in number, united with the Democratic minority to overrule a formal decision of the Speaker. A four days' parliamentary battle resulted, culminating in a reorganization of the all-powerful Rules Committee, with the Speaker no longer a member of it. The right of the Speaker to appoint this committee was also taken away. When the Democrats came into control of the House in 1911, they completed the dethronement of the Speaker by depriving him of the appointment of all committees.

The old system had not been without its advantages, when the power of the Speaker and his small group of associate party leaders was not abused. It at least concentrated responsibility in a few prominent members of the majority party. But it made it possible for these few men to perpetuate a machine and to ignore the desires of the rest of the party representatives and of the voters of the party throughout the country. The defeat of Cannonism put an end to the autocratic power of the Speaker and relegated him to the position of a mere presiding officer. It had also a wider significance, for it portended the division in the old Republican party out of which was to come the new Progressive party.

When the mid-point of the Taft Administration was reached, a practical test was given of the measure of popular approval which the President and his party associates had achieved. The congressional elections went decidedly against the Republicans. The Republican majority of forty-seven in the House was changed to a Democratic majority of fifty-four. The Republican majority in the Senate was cut down from twenty-eight to ten. Not only were the Democrats successful in this substantial degree, but many of the Western States elected Progressive Republicans instead of Republicans of the old type. During the last two years of his term, the President was consequently obliged to work with a Democratic House and with a Senate in which Democrats and Insurgent Republicans predominated over the old-line Republicans.

The second half of Taft's Presidency was productive of little but discord and dissatisfaction. The Democrats in power in the House were quite ready to harass the Republican President, especially in view of the approaching Presidential election. The Insurgents in House and Senate were not entirely unwilling to take a hand in the same game. Besides, they found themselves more and more in sincere disagreement with the President on matters of fundamental policy, though not one of them could fairly question his integrity of purpose, impugn his purity of character, or deny his charm of personality.

Three weeks after Taft's inauguration, Roosevelt sailed for Africa, to be gone for a year hunting big game. He went with a warm feeling of friendship and admiration for the man whom he had done so much to make President. He had high confidence that Taft would be successful in his great office. He had no reason to believe that any change would come in the friendship between them, which had been peculiarly intimate. From the steamer on which he sailed for Africa, he sent a long telegram of cordial and hearty good wishes to his successor in Washington.

The next year Roosevelt came back to the United States, after a triumphal tour of the capitals of Europe, to find his party disrupted and the progressive movement in danger of shipwreck. He had no intention of entering politics again. But he had no intention, either, of ceasing to champion the things in which he believed. This he made obvious, in his first speech after his return, to the cheering thousands who welcomed him at the Battery. He said:

"I have thoroughly enjoyed myself; and now I am more glad than I can say to get home, to be back in my own country, back among people I love. And I am ready and eager to do my part so far as I am able, in helping solve problems which must be solved, if we of this, the greatest democratic republic upon which the sun has ever shone, are to see its destinies rise to the high level of our hopes and its opportunities. This is the duty of every citizen, but is peculiarly my duty; for any man who has ever been honored by being made President of the United States is thereby forever rendered the debtor of the American people and is bound throughout his life to remember this, his prime obligation."

The welcome over, Roosevelt tried to take up the life of a private citizen. He had become Contributing Editor of The Outlook and had planned to give his energies largely to writing. But he was not to be let alone. The people who loved him demanded that they be permitted to see and to hear him. Those who were in the thick of the political fight on behalf of progress and righteousness called loudly to him for aid. Only a few days after Roosevelt had landed from Europe, Governor Hughes of New York met him at the Commencement exercises at Harvard and urged him to help in the fight which the Governor was then making for a direct primary law. Roosevelt did not wish to enter the lists again until he had had more time for orientation; but he always found it difficult to refuse a plea for help on behalf of a good cause. He therefore sent a vigorous telegram to the Republican legislators at Albany urging them to support Governor Hughes and to vote for the primary bill. But the appeal went in vain: the Legislature was too thoroughly boss-ridden. This telegram, however, sounded a warning to the usurpers in the house of the Republican Penelope that the fingers of the returned Odysseus had not lost their prowess with the heroic bow.

During the summer of 1910, Roosevelt made a trip to the West and in a speech at Ossawattomie, Kansas, set forth what came to be described as the New Nationalism. It was his draft of a platform, not for himself, but for the nation. A few fragments from that speech will suggest what Roosevelt was thinking about in those days when the Progressive party was stirring in the womb. "At many stages in the advance of humanity, this conflict between the men who possess more than they have earned and the men who have earned more than they possess is the central condition of progress. In our day it appears as the struggle of free men to gain and hold the right of self-government as against the special interests, who twist the methods of free government into machinery for defeating the popular will. At every stage, and under all circumstances, the essence of the struggle is to equalize opportunity, destroy privilege, and give to the life and citizenship of every individual the highest possible value both to himself and to the commonwealth.

"Every special interest is entitled to justice, but not one is entitled to a vote in Congress, to a voice on the bench, or to representation in any public office. The Constitution guarantees protection to property, and we must make that promise good. But it does not give the right of suffrage to any corporation.

"The absence of effective state and, especially, national restraint upon unfair money getting has tended to create a small class of enormously wealthy and economically powerful men, whose chief object is to hold and increase their power. The prime need is to change the conditions which enable these men to accumulate power which it is not for the general welfare that they should hold or exercise.

"We are face to face with new conceptions of the relations of property to human welfare, chiefly because certain advocates of the rights of property as against the rights of men have been pushing their claims too far.

"The State must be made efficient for the work which concerns only the people of the State; and the nation for that which concerns all the people. There must remain no neutral ground to serve as a refuge for lawbreakers, and especially for lawbreakers of great wealth, who can hire the vulpine legal cunning which will teach them how to avoid both jurisdictions.

"I do not ask for overcentralization; but I do ask that we work in a spirit of broad and far-reaching nationalism when we work for what concerns our people as a whole.

"We must have the right kind of character--character that makes a man, first of all, a good man in the home, a good father, a good husband--that makes a man a good neighbor.... The prime problem of our nation is to get the right kind of good citizenship, and to get it, we must have progress, and our public men must be genuinely progressive.

"I stand for the Square Deal. But when I say that I am for the square deal I mean not merely that I stand for fair play under the present rules of the game, but that I stand for having those rules changed so as to work for a more substantial equality of opportunity and of reward for equally good service."

These generalizations Roosevelt accompanied by specific recommendations. They included proposals for publicity of corporate affairs; prohibition of the use of corporate funds, for political purposes; governmental supervision of the capitalization of all corporations doing an interstate business; control and supervision of corporations and combinations controlling necessaries of life; holding the officers and directors of corporations personally liable when any corporation breaks the law; an expert tariff commission and revision of the tariff schedule by schedule; a graduated income tax and a graduated inheritance tax, increasing rapidly in amount with the size of the estate; conservation of natural resources and their use for the benefit of all rather than their monopolization for the benefit of the few; public accounting for all campaign funds before election; comprehensive workmen's compensation acts, state and national laws to regulate child labor and work for women, the enforcement of sanitary conditions for workers and the compulsory use of safety appliances in industry.

There was nothing in all these proposals that should have seemed revolutionary or extreme. But there was much that disturbed the reactionaries who were thinking primarily in terms of property and only belatedly or not at all of human rights. The Bourbons in the Republican party and their supporters among the special interests "viewed with, alarm" this frank attack upon their intrenched privileges. The Progressives, however, welcomed with eagerness this robust leadership. The breach in the Republican party was widening with steadily accelerating speed.

In the fall of 1910 a new demand arose that Roosevelt should enter actively into politics. Though it came from his own State, he resisted it with energy and determination. Nevertheless the pressure from his close political associates in New York finally became too much for him, and he yielded. They wanted him to go as a delegate to the Republican State Convention at Saratoga and to be a candidate for Temporary Chairman of the Convention--the officer whose opening speech is traditionally presumed to sound the keynote of the campaign. Roosevelt went and, after a bitter fight with the reactionists in the party, led by William Barnes of Albany, was elected Temporary Chairman over Vice-President James S. Sherman. The keynote was sounded in no uncertain tones, while Mr. Barnes and his associates fidgeted and suffered.

Then came a Homeric conflict, with a dramatic climax. The reactionary gang did not know that it was beaten. Its members resisted stridently an attempt to write a direct primary plank into the party platform. They wished to rebuke Governor Hughes, who was as little to their liking as Roosevelt himself, and they did not want the direct primary. After speeches by young James Wadsworth, later United States Senator, Job Hedges, and Barnes himself, in which they bewailed the impending demise of representative government and the coming of mob rule, it was clear that the primary plank was defeated. Then rose Roosevelt. In a speech that lashed and flayed the forces of reaction and obscurantism, he demanded that the party stand by the right of the people to rule. Single-handed he drove a majority of the delegates into line. The plank was adopted. Thenceforward the convention was his. It selected, as candidate for Governor, Henry W. Stimson, who had been a Federal attorney in New York under Roosevelt and Secretary of War in Taft's Cabinet. When this victory had been won, Roosevelt threw himself into the campaign with his usual abandon and toured the State, making fighting speeches in scores of cities and towns. But in spite of Roosevelt's best efforts, Stimson was defeated.

All this active participation in local political conflicts seriously distressed many of Roosevelt's friends and associates. They felt that he was too big to fritter himself away on small matters from which he--and the cause whose great champion he was--had so little to gain and so much to lose. They wanted him to wait patiently for the moment of destiny which they felt sure would come. But it was never easy for Roosevelt to wait. It was the hardest thing in the world for him to decline an invitation to enter a fight--when the cause was a righteous one.

So the year 1911 passed by, with the Taft Administration steadily losing prestige, and the revolt of the Progressives within the Republican party continually gathering momentum. Then came 1912, the year of the Glorious Failure.

# CHAPTER XIII. THE PROGRESSIVE PARTY

The Progressive party and the Progressive movement were two things. The one was born on a day, lived a stirring, strenuous span of life, suffered its fatal wound, lingered on for a few more years, and received its coup de grace. The other sprang like a great river system from a multitude of sources, flowed onward by a hundred channels, always converging and uniting, until a single mighty stream emerged to water and enrich and serve a broad country and a great people. The one was ephemeral, abortive--a failure. The other was permanent, creative--a triumph. The two were inseparable, each indispensable to the other. Just as the party would never have existed if there had been no movement, so the movement would not have attained such a surpassing measure of achievement so swiftly without the party.

The Progressive party came into full being at the convention held in Chicago on August 5, 1912 under dramatic circumstances. Every drama must have a beginning and this one had opened for the public when, on the 10th of February in the same year, the Republican Governors of West Virginia, Nebraska, New Hampshire, Wyoming, Michigan, Kansas, and Missouri addressed a letter to Roosevelt, in which they declared that, in considering what would best insure the continuation of the Republican party as a useful agency of good government, they had reached the conclusion that a large majority of the Republican voters of the country favored Roosevelt's nomination, and a large majority of the people favored his election as the next President. They asserted their belief that, in view of this public demand, he should soon declare whether, if the nomination came to him unsolicited and unsought, he would accept it. They concluded their request with this paragraph:

"In submitting this request we are not considering your personal interests. We do not regard it as proper to consider either the interest or the preference of any man as regards the nomination for the Presidency. We are expressing our sincere belief and best judgment as to what is demanded of you in the interests of the people as a whole. And we feel that you would be unresponsive to a plain public duty if you should decline to accept the nomination, coming as the voluntary expression of the wishes of a majority of the Republican voters of the United States, through the action of their delegates in the next National Convention."

The sincerity and whole-heartedness of the convictions here expressed are in no wise vitiated by the fact that the letter was not written until the seven Governors were assured what the answer to it would be. For the very beginning of our drama, then, we must go back a little farther to that day in late January of 1912 when Theodore Roosevelt himself came face to face with a momentous decision. On that day he definitely determined that his duty to the things in which he profoundly believed--and no less to the friends and associates who shared his beliefs--constrained him once more to enter the arena of political conflict and lead the fight.

Roosevelt had come to this conclusion with extreme reluctance. He had no illusions as to the probable effect upon his personal fortunes. Twice he had been President once by the hand of fate, once by a great popular vote. To be President again could add nothing to his prestige or fame; it could only subject him for four years to the dangerous vagaries of the unstable popular mood. He had nothing to gain for himself by entering the ring of political conflict again; the chances for personal loss were great. His enemies, his critics, and his political adversaries would have it that he was eaten up with ambition, that he came back from his African and European trip eager to thrust himself again into the limelight of national political life and to demand for himself again a great political prize. But his friends, his associates, and those who, knowing him at close range, understood him, realized that this was no picture of the truth. He accepted what hundreds of Progressive leaders and followers throughout the country--for the man in the ranks had as ready access to him as the most prominent leader, and received as warm consideration--asserted was his clear duty and obligation.

A letter which he had written two days before Christmas, 1911, shows unmistakably how his mind was working in those days of prologue to the great decision. The letter was entirely private, and was addressed to my father who was a publisher and a friend and not a politician. There is, therefore, no reason whatever why the letter should not be accepted as an accurate picture of Mr. Roosevelt's mind at that time: "Now for the message Harold gave me, that I should write you a little concerning political conditions. They are very, very mixed. Curiously enough, my article on the trusts was generally accepted as bringing me forward for the Presidential nomination. Evidently what really happened was that there had been a strong undercurrent of feeling about me, and that the talk concerning the article enabled this feeling to come to the surface. I do not think it amounts to anything. It merely means that a great many people do not get the leadership they are looking for from any of the prominent men in public life, and that under the circumstances they grasp at any one; and as my article on the McNamaras possessed at least the merit of being entirely clearcut and of showing that I knew my own mind and had definite views, a good many plain people turned longingly to me as a leader. Taft is very weak, but La Follette has not developed real strength east of the Mississippi River, excepting of course in Wisconsin. West of the River he has a large following, although there is a good deal of opposition to him even in States like Kansas, Washington, and California. East of the Mississippi, I believe he can only pick up a few delegates here and there. Taft will have most of the Southern delegates, he will have the officeholders, and also the tepid and acquiescent, rather than active, support of the ordinary people who do not feel very strongly one way or the other, and who think it is the usual thing to renominate a President. If there were a strong candidate against him, he would I believe be beaten, but there are plenty of men, many of the leaders not only here but in Texas, for instance, in Ohio, in New Hampshire and Illinois, who are against him, but who are even more against La Follette, and who regard themselves as limited to the alternative between the two. There is, of course, always the danger that there may be a movement for me, the danger coming partly because the men who may be candidates are very anxious that the ticket shall be strengthened and care nothing for the fate of the man who strengthens it, and partly because there is a good deal of honest feeling for me among plain simple people who wish leadership, but who will not accept leadership unless they believe it to be sincere, fearless, and intelligent. I most emphatically do not wish the nomination. Personally I should regard it as a calamity to be nominated. In the first place, I might very possibly be beaten, and in the next place, even if elected I should be confronted with almost impossible conditions out of which to make good results. In the tariff, for instance, I would have to face the fact that men would keep comparing what I did, not with what the Democrats would or could have done but with an ideal, or rather with a multitude of entirely separate and really incompatible ideals. I am not a candidate, I will never be a candidate; but I have to tell the La Follette men and the Taft men that while I am absolutely sincere in saying that I am not a candidate and do not wish the nomination, yet that I do not feel it would be right or proper for me to say that under no circumstances would I accept it if it came; because, while wildly improbable, it is yet possible that there might be a public demand which would present the matter to me in the light of a duty which I could not shirk. In other words, while I emphatically do not want office, and have not the slightest idea that any demand for me will come, yet if there were a real public demand that in the public interest I should do a given job, it MIGHT be that I would not feel like flinching from the task. However, this is all in the air, and I do not for one moment believe that it will be necessary for me even to consider the matter. As for the Democrats, they have their troubles too. Wilson, although still the strongest man the Democrats could nominate, is much weaker than he was. He has given a good many people a feeling that he is very ambitious and not entirely sincere, and his demand for the Carnegie pension created an unpleasant impression. Harmon is a good old solid Democrat, with the standards of political and commercial morality of twenty years ago, who would be eagerly welcomed by all the conservative crowd. Champ Clark is a good fellow, but impossible as President.

"I think a good deal will depend upon what this Congress does. Taft may redeem himself. He was fairly strong at the end of the last session, but went off lamentably on account of his wavering and shillyshallying on so many matters during his speaking trip. His speeches generally hurt him, and rarely benefit him. But it is possible that the Democrats in Congress may play the fool, and give him the chance to appear as the strong leader, the man who must be accepted to oppose them."

This was what Roosevelt at the end, of December sincerely believed would be the situation as time went on. But he underestimated the strength and the volume of the tide that was rising.

The crucial decision was made on the 18th of January. I was in the closest possible touch with Roosevelt in those pregnant days, and I know, as well as any but the man himself could know, how his mind was working. An entry in my diary on that date shows the origin of the letter of the seven governors:

"Senator Beveridge called on T. R. to urge him to make a public statement soon. T. R. impressed by his arguments and by letters just received from three Governors, Hadley, Glasscock, and Bass. Practically determined to ask these Governors, and Stubbs and Osborne, to send him a joint letter asking him to make a public state-ment to the effect that if there is a genuine popular demand for his nomination he will not refuse-in other words to say to him in a joint letter for publication just what they have each said to him in private letters. Such joint action would give him a proper reason--or occasion--for making a public declaration. T. R. telegraphed Frank Knox, Republican State Chairman of Michigan and former member of his regiment, to come down, with intention of asking him to see the various governors. H. H., at Ernest Abbott's suggestion, asked him not to make final decision till he has had conference--already arranged--with editorial staff. T. R. agrees, but the inevi-tableness of the matter is evident."

After that day, things moved rapidly. Two days later the diary contains this re-cord: "Everett Colby, William Fellowes Morgan, and Mark Sullivan call on T. R. All inclined to agree that time for statement is practically here. T. R.--The time to use a man is when the people want to use him." M. S.--"The time to set a hen is when the hen wants to set." Frank Knox comes in response to telegram. Nat Wright also present at interview where Knox is informed of the job proposed for him. Gifford Pinchot also present at beginning of interview while T. R. tells how he views the situation, but leaves (at T. R.'s suggestion) before real business of conference begins. Plan outlined to Knox, who likes it, and subsequently, in H. H.'s office, draws up letter for Governors. Draft shown to T. R., who suggests a couple of added sentences emphasizing that the nomination must come as a real popular demand, and declar-ing that the Governors are taking their action not for his sake, but for the sake of the country. Knox takes copy of letter and starts for home, to go out to see Governors as soon as possible.

On the 22d of January the Conference with The Outlook editorial staff took place and is thus described in my diary:

"T. R. had long conference with entire staff. All except R. D. T. [Mr. Townsend, Managing Editor of The Outlook] and H. H. inclined to deprecate a public state-ment now. T. R.--'I have had all the honor the American public can give me. If I should be elected I would go back not so young as I once was, with all the first fine flavor gone, and take up the horrible task of going in and out, in and out, of the same hole over and over again. But I cannot decline the call. Too many of those who have fought with me the good fight for the things we believe in together, declare that at this critical moment I am the instrument that ought to be used to make it possible for me to refuse. I BELIEVE I SHALL BE BROKEN IN THE USING. But I cannot refuse to permit myself to be used. I am not going to get those good fellows out on the end of a limb and then saw off the limb.' R. D. T. suggested that it be said frankly that the Governors wrote the joint letter at T. R.'s request. T. R. accepted like a shot. Went into H. H.'s room, dictated two or three sentences to that effect, which H. H. later incorporated in letter. [This plan was later given up, I believe on the urging of some or all of the Governors involved.] T. R.--'I can't go on telling my friends in private letters what my position is, but asking them not to make it public, without seeming furtive.' In afternoon H. H. suggests that T. R. write first draft of his letter of reply soon as possible to give all possible time for consideration and revision. T. R. has two inspirations--to propose presidential primaries in order to be sure of popular demand, and to use statement made at Battery when he returned home from Europe."

The next day's entry reads as follows:

"Sent revised letter to Knox. T. R. said, "Not to make a public statement soon would be to violate my cardinal principle--never hit if you can help it, but when you have to, hit hard. NEVER hit soft. You'll never get any thanks for hitting soft." McHarg called with three men from St. Louis. T. R. said exactly the same thing as usual--he would never accept the nomination if it came as the result of an intrigue, only if it came as the result of a genuine and widespread popular demand. The thing he wants to be sure of is that there is this widespread popular demand that he "do a job," and that the demand is genuine."

Meanwhile Frank Knox was consulting the seven Governors, each one of whom was delighted to have an opportunity to say to Roosevelt in this formal, public way just what they had each said to him privately and forcefully. The letter was signed and delivered to T. R. On the 24th of February Roosevelt replied to the letter of the seven Governors in unequivocal terms, "I will accept the nomination for President if it is tendered to me, and I will adhere to this decision until--the convention has expressed its preference." He added the hope that so far as possible the people might be given the chance, through direct primaries, to record their wish as to who should be the nominee. A month later, in a great address at Carnegie Hall in New York, he gave voice publicly to the same thought that he had expressed to his friends in that editorial conference: "The leader for the time being, whoever he may be, is but an instrument, to be used until broken and then cast aside; and if he is worth his salt he will care no more when he is broken than a soldier cares when he is sent where his life is forfeit that the victory may be won. In the long fight for righteousness the watchword for all is, 'Spend and be spent.' It is of little matter whether any one man fails or succeeds; but the cause shall not fail, for it is the cause of mankind."

The decision once made, Roosevelt threw himself into the contest for delegates to the nominating convention with his unparalleled vigor and forcefulness. His main opponent was, of course, the man who had been his friend and associate and whom he had done more than any other single force to make President as his successor. William Howard Taft had the undivided support of the national party organization; but the Progressive Republicans the country over thronged to Roosevelt's support with wild enthusiasm. The campaign for the nomination quickly developed two aspects, one of which delighted every Progressive in the Republican party, the other of which grieved every one of Roosevelt's levelheaded friends. It became a clean-cut conflict between progress and reaction, between the interests of the people, both as rulers and as governed, and the special interests, political and business. But it also became a bitter conflict of personalities between the erstwhile friends. The breach between the two men was afterwards healed, but it was several years after the reek of the battle had drifted away before even formal relations were restored between them.

A complicating factor in the campaign was the candidacy of Senator La Follette of Wisconsin. In July, 1911, La Follette had begun, at the earnest solicitation of many Progressive leaders in Congress and out, an active campaign for the Republican nomination. Progressive organizations were perfected in numerous States and "in less than three months," as La Follette has written in his Autobiography, his candidacy "had taken on proportions which compelled recognition." Four months later a conference of some three hundred Progressives from thirty States, meeting in Chicago, declared that La Follette was, because of his record, the logical candidate for the Presidency. Following this conference he continued to campaign with increasing vigor, but concurrently the enthusiasm of some of his leading supporters began to cool and their support of his candidacy to weaken. Senator La Follette ascribes this effect to the surreptitious maneuvering of Roosevelt, whom he credits with an overwhelming appetite for another Presidential term, kept in check only by his fear that he could not be nominated or elected. But there is no evidence of any value whatever that Roosevelt was conducting underground operations or that he desired to be President again. The true explanation of the change in those Progressives who had favored the candidacy of La Follette and yet had gradually ceased to support him, is to be found in their growing conviction that Taft and the reactionary forces in the Republican party which he represented could be defeated only by one man--and that not the Senator from Wisconsin. In any event the La Follette candidacy rapidly declined until it ceased to be a serious element in the situation. Although the Senator, with characteristic consistency and pertinacity, stayed in the fight till the end, he entered the Convention with the delegates of but two States, his own Wisconsin and North Dakota, pledged to support him.

The pre-convention campaign was made unusually dramatic by the fact that, for the first time in the history of Presidential elections, the voters of thirteen States were privileged not only to select the delegates to the Convention by direct primary vote but to instruct them in the same way as to the candidate for whom they should cast their ballots. There were 388 such popularly instructed delegates from California, Georgia, Illinois, Maryland, Massachusetts, Nebraska, New Jersey, North Dakota, Ohio, Oregon, Pennsylvania, South Dakota, and Wisconsin. It was naturally in these States that the two candidates concentrated their campaigning efforts. The result of the selection of delegates and of the preferential vote in these States was the best possible evidence of the desire of the rank and file of the party as to the Presidential candidate. Of these 388 delegates, Senator La Follette secured 36; President Taft 71--28 in Georgia, 2 in Illinois, 18 in Massachusetts, 14 in Ohio, and 9 in Pennsylvania; and Roosevelt 281--26 in California, 56 in Illinois, 16 in Maryland, 18 in Massachusetts, 16 in Nebraska, 28 in New Jersey, 34 in Ohio, 10 in Oregon, 67 in Pennsylvania, and 10 in South Dakota. Roosevelt therefore, in those States where the voters could actually declare at primary elections which candidate they preferred, was the expressed choice of more than five times as many voters as Taft.

When the Republican convention met in Chicago an interesting and peculiar situation presented itself. There were 1078 seats in the Convention. Of the delegates elected to those seats Taft had committed to him the vast majority of the delegates from the States which have never cast an electoral vote for a Republican candidate for President since there was a Republican party. Roosevelt had in support of him the great majority of the delegates from the States which are normally Republican and which must be relied upon at election time if a Republican President is to be chosen. Of the 1078 seats more than 200 were contested. Aside from these contested seats, neither candidate had a majority of the delegates. The problem that confronted each side was to secure the filling of a sufficient number of the disputed seats with its retainers to insure a majority for its candidate. In the solution of this problem the Taft forces had one insuperable advantage. The temporary roll of a nominating convention is made up by the National Committee of the party. The Republican National Committee had been selected at the close of the last national convention four years before. It accordingly represented the party as it had then stood, regardless of the significant changes that three and a quarter years of Taft's Presidency had wrought in party opinion.

In the National Committee the Taft forces had a strength of more than two to one; and all but an insignificant number of the contests were decided out of hand in favor of Mr. Taft. The temporary roll of the Convention therefore showed a distinct majority against Roosevelt. From the fall of the gavel, the Roosevelt forces fought with vigor and determination for what they described as the "purging of the roll" of those Taft delegates whose names they declared had been placed upon it by fraud. But at every turn the force of numbers was against them; and the Taft majority which the National Committee had constituted in the Convention remained intact, an impregnable defense against the Progressive attack.

These preliminary engagements concerned with the determination of the final membership of the Convention had occupied several days. Meanwhile the temper of the Roosevelt delegates had burned hotter and hotter. Roosevelt was present, leading the fight in person--not, of course, on the floor of the Convention, to which he was not a delegate, but at headquarters in the Congress Hotel. There were not wanting in the Progressive forces counsels of moderation and compromise. It was suggested by those of less fiery mettle that harmony might be arrived at on the basis of the elimination of both Roosevelt and Taft and the selection of a candidate not unsatisfactory to either side. But Roosevelt, backed by the majority of the Progressive delegates, stood firm and immovable on the ground that the "roll must be purged" and that he would consent to no traffic with a Convention whose make-up contained delegates holding their seats by virtue of fraud. "Let them purge the roll," he declared again and again, "and I will accept any candidate the Convention may name." But the organization leaders knew that a yielding to this demand for a reconstitution of the personnel of the Convention would result in but one thing--the nomination for Roosevelt--and this was the one thing they were resolved not to permit.

As the hours of conflict and turmoil passed, there grew steadily and surely in the Roosevelt ranks a demand for a severance of relations with the fraudulent Convention and the formation of a new party devoted, without equivocation or compromise, to Progressive principles. A typical incident of these days of confusion and uncertainty was the drawing up of a declaration of purpose by a Progressive alternate from New Jersey, disgusted with the progress of the machine steam roller and disappointed at the delayed appearance of a positive Progressive programme of action. Circulated privately, with the knowledge and approval of Roosevelt, it was promptly signed by dozens of Progressive delegates. It read as follows:

"We, the undersigned, in the event that the Republican National Convention as at present constituted refuses to purge its roll of the delegates fraudulently placed upon it by the action of the majority of the Republican National Committee, pledge ourselves, as American citizens devoted to the progressive principles of genuine popular rule and social justice, to join in the organization of a new party founded upon those principles, under the leadership of Theodore Roosevelt."

The first signer of the declaration was Governor Hiram W. Johnson of California, the second, Governor Robert S. Vessey of South Dakota, the third, Governor Joseph M. Carey of Wyoming, and farther down the list were the names of Gifford and Amos Pinchot, James R. Garfield, ex-Governor John Franklin Fort of New Jersey, with Everett Colby and George L. Record of the same State, Matthew Hale of Massachusetts, "Jack" Greenway of Arizona, Judge Ben B. Lindsey of Colorado, Medill McCormick of Illinois, George Rublee of New Hampshire, and Elon Huntington Hooker, of New York, who was to become the National Treasurer of the new party. The document was, of course, a purely informal assertion of purpose; but it was the first substantial straw to predict the whirlwind which the masters of the convention were to reap.

When at last it had become unmistakably clear that the Taft forces were and would remain to the end in control of the Convention, the Progressive delegates, with a few exceptions, united in dramatic action. Speaking for them with passion and intensity Henry J. Allen of Kansas announced their intention to participate no longer in the actions of a convention vitiated by fraud. The Progressive delegates would, he declared, remain in their places but they would neither vote nor take any part whatever in the proceedings. He then read, by permission of the Convention, a statement from Roosevelt, in which he pronounced the following indictment:

"The Convention has now declined to purge the roll of the fraudulent delegates placed thereon by the defunct National Committee, and the majority which has thus indorsed the fraud was made a majority only because it included the fraudulent delegates themselves who all sat as judges on one another's cases.... The Convention as now composed has no claim to represent the voters of the Republican party.... Any man nominated by the Convention as now constituted would merely be the beneficiary of this successful fraud; it would be deeply discreditable for any man to accept the Convention's nomination under these circumstances; and any man thus accepting it would have no claim to the support of any Republican on party grounds and would have forfeited the right to ask the support of any honest man of any party on moral grounds."

So while most of the Roosevelt delegates sat in ominous quiet and refused to vote, the Convention proceeded to nominate Taft for President by the following vote: Taft 561--21 votes more than a majority; Roosevelt 107; La Follette 41; Cummins 17; Hughes 2; absent 6; present and not voting 344.

Then the Taft delegates went home to meditate on the fight which they had won and the more portentous fight which they must wage in the coming months on a broader field. The Roosevelt delegates, on the other hand, went out to Orchestra Hall, and in an exalted mood of passionate devotion to their cause and their beloved leader proceeded to nominate Theodore Roosevelt for the Presidency and Hiram Johnson for the Vice-Presidency. A committee was sent to notify Roosevelt of the nomination and when he appeared in the hall all precedents of spontaneous enthusiasm were broken. This was no conventional--if the double entendre may be permitted--demonstration. It had rather the quality of religious exaltation.

Roosevelt made a short speech, in which he adjured his hearers to go to their several homes "to find out the sentiment of the people at home and then again come together, I suggest by mass convention, to nominate for the Presidency a Progressive on a Progressive platform that will enable us to appeal to Northerner and Southerner, Easterner and Westerner, Republican and Democrat alike, in the name of our common American citizenship. If you wish me to make the fight I will make it, even if only one State should support me."

Thus ended the first act in the drama. The second opened with the gathering of some two thousand men and women at Chicago on August 5, 1912. It was a unique gathering. Many of the delegates were women; one of the "keynote" speeches was delivered by Miss Jane Addams of Hull House. The whole tone and atmosphere of the occasion seemed religious rather than political. The old-timers among the delegates, who found themselves in the new party for diverse reasons, selfish, sincere, or mixed, must have felt astonishment at themselves as they stood and shouted out Onward Christian Soldiers as the battle-hymn of their new allegiance. The long address which Roosevelt made to the Convention he denominated his "Confession of Faith." The platform which the gathering adopted was entitled "A Contract with the People." The sessions of the Convention seethed with enthusiasm and burned hot with earnest devotion to high purpose. There could be no doubt in the mind of any but the most cynical of political reactionaries that here was the manifestation of a new and revivifying force to be reckoned with in the future development of American political life. The platform adopted by the Progressive Convention was no less a novelty. Its very title--even the fact that it had a title marked it off from the pompous and shopworn documents emanating from the usual nominating Convention--declared a reversal of the time-honored view of a platform as, like that of a street-car, "something to get in on, not something to stand on." The delegates to that Convention were perfectly ready to have their party sued before the bar of public opinion for breach of contract if their candidates when elected did not do everything in their power to carry out the pledges of the platform. The planks of the platform grouped themselves into three main sections: political reforms, control of trusts and combinations, and measures of "social and industrial justice."

In the first section were included direct primaries, nation-wide preferential primaries for the selection of candidates for the Presidency, direct popular election of United States Senators, the short ballot, the initiative, referendum and recall, an easier method of amending the Federal constitution, woman suffrage, and the recall of judicial decisions in the form of a popular review of any decision annulling a law passed under the police power of the State.

The platform in the second place opposed vigorously the indiscriminate dissolution of trusts and combinations, on the ground that combination in the business field was not only inevitable but necessary and desirable for the promotion of national and international efficiency. It condemned the evils of inflated capitalization and unfair competition; and it proposed, in order to eliminate those is evils while preserving the unquestioned advantages that flow from combination, the establishment of a strong Federal commission empowered and directed to maintain permanent active supervision over industrial corporations engaged in interstate commerce, doing for them what the Federal Government now does for the national banks and, through the Interstate Commerce Commission, for the transportation lines. Finally in the field of social justice the platform pledged the party to the abolition of child labor, to minimum wage laws, the eight-hour day, publicity in regard to working conditions, compensation for industrial accidents, continuation schools for industrial education, and to legislation to prevent industrial accidents, occupational diseases, overwork, involuntary unemployment, and other injurious effects incident to modern industry.

To stand upon this platform and to carry out the terms of this "contract with the people," the Convention nominated without debate or dissent Theodore Roosevelt for President and Hiram W. Johnson of California for Vice-President. Governor Johnson was an appropriate running mate for Roosevelt. In his own State he had led one of the most virile and fast moving of the local Progressive movements. He burned with a white-hot enthusiasm for the democratic ideal and the rights of man as embodied in equality of opportunity, freedom of individual development, and protection from the "dark forces" of special privilege, political autocracy and concentrated wealth. He was a brilliant and fiery campaigner where his convictions were enlisted.

So passed the second act in the drama of the Progressive party.

# CHAPTER XIV. THE GLORIOUS FAILURE

The third act in the drama of the Progressive party was filled with the campaign for the Presidency. It was a three-cornered fight. Taft stood for Republican conservatism and clung to the old things. Roosevelt fought for the progressive rewriting of Republican principles with added emphasis on popular government and social justice as defined in the New Nationalism. The Democratic party under the leadership of Woodrow Wilson espoused with more or less enthusiasm the old Democratic principles freshly interpreted and revivified in the declaration they called the New Freedom. The campaign marked the definite entrance of the nation upon a new era. One thing was clear from the beginning: the day of conservatism and reaction was over; the people of the United States had definitely crossed their Rubicon and had committed themselves to spiritual and moral progress.

The campaign had one dramatic incident. On the 14th of October, just before entering the Auditorium at Milwaukee, Roosevelt was shot by a fanatic. His immediate action was above everything characteristic. Some time later in reply to a remark that he had been foolhardy in going on with his speech just after the attack, Roosevelt said, "Why, you know, I didn't think I had been mortally wounded. If I had been mortally wounded, I would have bled from the lungs. When I got into the motor I coughed hard three times, and put my hand up to my mouth; as I did not find any blood, I thought that I was not seriously hurt, and went on with my speech."

The opening words of the speech which followed were equally typical:

"Friends, I shall ask you to be as quiet as possible. I don't know whether you fully understand that I have just been shot; but it takes more than that to kill a Bull Moose.... The bullet is in me now, so that I cannot make a very long speech, but

I will try my best.... First of all, I want to say this about myself; I have altogether too important things to think of to feel any concern over my own death; and now I cannot speak insincerely to you within five minutes of being shot. I am telling you the literal truth when I say that my concern is for many other things. It is not in the least for my own life. I want you to understand that I am ahead of the game anyway. No man has had a happier life than I have led; a happier life in every way. I have been able to do certain things that I greatly wished to do, and I am interested in doing other things. I can tell you with absolute truthfulness that I am very much uninterested in whether I am shot or not. It was just as when I was colonel of my regiment. I always felt that a private was to be excused for feeling at times some pangs of anxiety about his personal safety, but I cannot understand a man fit to be a colonel who can pay any heed to his personal safety when he is occupied as he ought to be occupied with the absorbing desire to do his duty."

There was a great deal of self-revelation in these words. Even the critic accustomed to ascribe to Roosevelt egotism and love of gallery applause must concede the courage, will-power, and self-forgetfulness disclosed by the incident.

The election was a debacle for reaction, a victory for Democracy, a triumph in defeat for the Progressive party. Taft carried two States, Utah and Vermont, with eight electoral votes; Woodrow Wilson carried forty States, with 435 electoral votes; and Roosevelt carried five States, Michigan, Minnesota, Pennsylvania, South Dakota, and Washington, and eleven out of the thirteen votes of California, giving him 88 electoral votes. Taft's popular vote was 3,484,956; Wilson's was 6,293,019; while Roosevelt's was 4,119,507. The fact that Wilson was elected by a minority popular vote is not the significant thing, for it is far beyond the capability of any political observer to declare what would have been the result if there had been but two parties in the field. The triumph for the Progressive party lay in the certainty that its emergence had compelled the election of a President whose face was toward the future. If the Roosevelt delegates at Chicago in June had acquiesced in the result of the steam-roller Convention, it is highly probable that Woodrow Wilson would not have been the choice of the Democratic Convention that met later at Baltimore.

During the succeeding four years the Progressive party, as a national organization, continued steadily to "dwindle, peak, and pine." More and more of its members and supporters slipped or stepped boldly back to the Republican party. Its quondam Democratic members had largely returned to their former allegiance with Wilson, either at the election or after it. Roosevelt once more withdrew from active participation in public life, until the Great War, with its gradually increasing intrusions upon American interests and American rights, aroused him to vigorous and aggressive utterance on American responsibility and American duty. He became a vigorous critic of the Administration.

Once more a demand began to spring up for his nomination for the Presidency; the Progressive party began to show signs of reviving consciousness. There had persisted through the years a little band of irreconcilables who were Progressives or nothing. They wanted a new party of radical ideas regardless of anything in the way of reformation and progress that the old parties might achieve. There were others who preferred to go back to the Republican party rather than to keep up the Progressive party as a mere minority party of protest, but who hoped in going back to be able to influence their old party along the lines of progress. There were those who were Rooseveltians pure and simple and who would follow him wherever he led.

All these groups wanted Roosevelt as President. They united to hold a convention of the Progressive party at Chicago in 1916 on the same days on which the Republican Convention met there. Each convention opened with a calculating eye upon the activities of the other. But both watched with even more anxious surmise for some sign of intention from the Progressive leader back at Oyster Bay. He held in his single hand the power of life and death for the Progressive party. His decision as to cooperative action with the Republicans or individual action as a Progressive would be the most important single factor in the campaign against Woodrow Wilson, who was certain of renomination. Three questions confronted and puzzled the two bodies of delegates: Would the Republicans nominate Roosevelt or another? If another, what would Roosevelt do? If another, what would the Progressives do?

For three days the Republican National Convention proceeded steadily and stolidly upon its appointed course. Everything had been done in the stereotyped way on the stereotyped time-table in the stereotyped language. No impropriety or infelicity had been permitted to mar the smooth texture of its surface. The temporary chairman in his keynote speech had been as mildly oratorical, as diffusely patriotic, and as nobly sentimental as any Fourth of July orator of a bygone day.

The whole tone of the Convention had been subdued and decorous with the decorum of incertitude and timidity. That Convention did not know what it wanted. It only knew that there was one thing that it did not want and that it was afraid of, and another thing it would rather not have and was afraid it would have to take. It wanted neither Theodore Roosevelt nor Charles E. Hughes, and its members were distinctly uncomfortable at the thought that they might have to take one or the other. It was an old-fashioned convention of the hand-picked variety. It smacked of the former days when the direct primary had not yet introduced the disturbing thought that the voters and not the office-holders and party leaders ought to select their candidates.

It was a docile, submissive convention, not because it was ruled by a strong group of men who knew what they wanted and proposed to compel their followers to give it to them, but because it was composed of politicians great and small to whom party regularity was the breath of their nostrils. They were ready to do the regular thing; but the only two things in sight were confoundedly irregular.

Two drafts were ready for their drinking and they dreaded both. They could nominate one of two men, and to nominate either of them was to fling open the gates of the citadel of party regularity and conformity and let the enemy in. Was it to be Roosevelt or Hughes? Roosevelt they would not have. Hughes they would give their eye teeth not to take. No wonder they were subdued and inarticulate. No wonder they suffered and were unhappy. So they droned along through their stereotyped routine, hoping dully against fate.

The hot-heads in the Progressive Convention wanted no delay, no compromise. They would have nominated Theodore Roosevelt out of hand with a whoop, and let the Republican Convention take him or leave him. But the cooler leaders realized the importance of union between the two parties and knew, or accurately guessed, what the attitude of Roosevelt would be. With firm hand they kept the Convention from hasty and irrevocable action. They proposed that overtures be made to the Republican Convention with a view to harmonious agreement. A conference was held between committees of the two conventions to see if common ground could be discovered. At the first session of the joint committee it appeared that there was sincere desire on both sides to get together, but that the Progressives would have no one but Roosevelt, while the Republicans would not have him but were united on no one else. When the balloting began in the Republican Convention, the only candidate who received even a respectable block of votes was Hughes, but his total was hardly more than half of the necessary majority. For several ballots there was no considerable gain for any of the numerous candidates, and when the Convention adjourned late Friday night the outcome was as uncertain as ever. But by Saturday morning the Republican leaders and delegates had resigned themselves to the inevitable, and the nomination of Hughes was assured. When the Progressive Convention met that morning, the conference committee reported that the Republican members of the committee had proposed unanimously the selection of Hughes as the candidate of both parties.

Thus began the final scene in the Progressive drama, and a more thrilling and intense occasion it would be difficult to imagine. It was apparent that the Progressive delegates would have none of it. They were there to nominate their own beloved leader and they intended to do it. A telegram was received from Oyster Bay proposing Senator Lodge as the compromise candidate, and the restive delegates in the Auditorium could with the greatest difficulty be held back until the telegram could be received and read at the Coliseum. A direct telephone wire from the Coliseum to a receiver on the stage of the Auditorium kept the Progressive body in instant touch with events in the other Convention. In the Auditorium the atmosphere was electric. The delegates bubbled with excitement. They wanted to nominate Roosevelt and be done with it. The fear that the other Convention would steal a march on them and make its nomination first set them crazy with impatience. The hall rumbled and sputtered and fizzed and detonated. The floor looked like a giant corn popper with the kernels jumping and exploding like mad.

The delegates wanted action; the leaders wanted to be sure that they had kept faith with Roosevelt and with the general situation by giving the Republican delegates a chance to hear his last proposal. Bainbridge Colby, of New York, put Roosevelt in nomination with brevity and vigor; Hiram Johnson seconded the nomination with his accustomed fire. Then, as the word came over the wire that balloting had been resumed in the Coliseum, the question was put at thirty-one minutes past twelve, and every delegate and every alternate in the Convention leaped to his feet with upstretched arm and shouted "Aye."

Doubtless more thrilling moments may come to some men at some time, somewhere, but you will hardly find a delegate of that Progressive Convention to believe it. Then the Convention adjourned, to meet again at three to hear what the man they had nominated would say.

At five o'clock in the afternoon, after a couple of hours of impatient and anxious marking time with routine matters, the Progressive delegates received the reply from their leader. It read thus:

"I am very grateful for the honor you confer upon me by nominating me as President. I cannot accept it at this time. I do not know the attitude of the candidate of the Republican party toward the vital questions of the day. Therefore, if you desire an immediate decision, I must decline the nomination.

"But if you prefer to wait, I suggest that my conditional refusal to run be placed in the hands of the Progressive National Committee. If Mr. Hughes's statements, when he makes them, shall satisfy the committee that it is for the interest of the country that he be elected, they can act accordingly and treat my refusal as definitely accepted.

"If they are not satisfied, they can so notify the Progressive party, and at the same time they can confer with me, and then determine on whatever action we may severally deem appropriate to meet the needs of the country.

"THEODORE ROOSEVELT."

Puzzled, disheartened, overwhelmed, the Progressive delegates went away. They could not then see how wise, how farsighted, how inevitable Roosevelt's decision was. Some of them will never see it. Probably few of them as they went out of those doors realized that they had taken part in the last act of the romantic and tragic drama of the National Progressive party. But such was the fact, for the march of events was too much for it. Fate, not its enemies, brought it to an end.

So was born, lived a little space, and died the Progressive party. At its birth it caused the nomination, by the Democrats, and the election, by the people, of Woodrow Wilson. At its death it brought about the nomination of Charles E. Hughes by the Republicans. It forced the writing into the platforms of the more conservative parties of principles and programmes of popular rights and social regeneration. The Progressive party never attained to power, but it wielded a potent power. It was a glorious failure.

# CHAPTER XV. THE FIGHTING EDGE

Theodore Roosevelt was a prodigious coiner of phrases. He added scores of them, full of virility, picturesqueness, and flavor to the every-day speech of the American people. They stuck, because they expressed ideas that needed expressing and because they expressed them so well that no other combinations of words could quite equal them. One of the best, though not the most popular, of his phrases is contained in the following quotation:

"One of the prime dangers of civilization has always been its tendency to cause the loss of virile fighting virtues, of the fighting edge. When men get too comfortable and lead too luxurious lives, there is always danger lest the softness eat like an acid into their manliness of fiber."

He used the same phrase many times. Here is another instance:

"Unjust war is to be abhorred; but woe to the nation that does not make ready to hold its own in time of need against all who would harm it! And woe, thrice over, to the nation in which the average man loses the fighting edge, loses the power to serve as a soldier if the day of need should arise!"

That was it--THE FIGHTING EDGE. Roosevelt had it, if ever man had. The conviction of the need for that combination of physical and spiritual qualities that this represented, if a man is to take his place and keep it in the world, became an inseparable part of his consciousness early in life. It grew in strength and depth with every year that he lived. He learned the need of preparedness on that day in Maine when he found himself helpless before the tormenting of his young fellow travelers. In the gymnasium on Twentieth Street, within the boxing ring at Harvard, in the New York Assembly, in the conflicts with the spoilsmen in Washington, on the frontier in cowboy land, in Mulberry Street and on Capitol Hill, and in the jungle before Santiago, the lesson was hammered into him by the stern reality of events.

The strokes fell on malleable metal.

In the spring of 1897, Roosevelt had been appointed Assistant Secretary of the Navy, largely through the efforts of his friend, Senator Henry Cabot Lodge of Massachusetts. The appointment was excellent from every point of view. Though Roosevelt had received no training for the post so far as technical education was concerned, he brought to his duties a profound belief in the navy and a keen interest in its development. His first published book had been "The Naval War of 1812"; and the lessons of that war had not been lost upon him. It was indeed a fortuitous circumstance that placed him in this branch of the national service just as relations between Spain and the United States were reaching the breaking point. When the battleship Maine was sunk in Havana Harbor, his reaction to that startling event was instantaneous. He was convinced that the sinking of the Maine made war inevitable, but he had long been certain that war ought to come. He believed that the United States had a moral duty toward the Cuban people, oppressed, abused, starved, and murdered at the hands of Spain.

He was not the head of the Navy Department, but that made little difference. The Secretary was a fine old gentleman, formerly president of the Massachusetts Peace Society, and by temperament indisposed to any rapid moves toward war. But he liked his Assistant Secretary and did not put too stern a curb upon his impetuous activity and Roosevelt's activity was vigorous and unceasing. Secretary Long has described it, rather with justice than with enthusiasm.

"His activity was characteristic. He was zealous in the work of putting the navy in condition for the apprehended struggle. His ardor sometimes went faster than the President or the Department approved.... He worked indefatigably, frequently incorporating his views in memoranda which he would place every morning on my desk. Most of his suggestions had, however, so far as applicable, been already adopted by the various bureaus, the chiefs of which were straining every nerve and leaving nothing undone. When I suggested to him that some future historian reading his memoranda, if they were put on record, would get the impression that the bureaus were inefficient, he accepted the suggestion with the generous good nature which is so marked in him. Indeed, nothing could be pleasanter than our relations. He was heart and soul in his work. His typewriters had no rest. He, like most of us, lacks the rare knack of brevity. He was especially stimulating to the younger officers who gathered about him and made his office as busy as a hive. He was especially helpful in the purchasing of ships and in every line where he could push on the work of preparation for war."

One suspects that the Secretary may have been more complacently convinced of the forehandedness of the bureau chiefs than was his impatient associate. For, while the navy was apparently in better shape than the army in those days, there must have been, even in the Department where Roosevelt's typewriters knew no rest, some of that class of desk-bound officers whom he met later when he was organizing the Rough Riders. His experience with one such officer in the War Department was humorous. This bureaucrat was continually refusing Roosevelt's applications because they were irregular. In each case Roosevelt would appeal to the Secretary of War, with whom he was on the best of terms, and would get from him an order countenancing the irregularity. After a number of experiences of this kind, the harassed slave of red tape threw himself back in his chair and exclaimed, "Oh, dear! I had this office running in such good shape--and then along came the war and upset everything!"

But there were plenty of good men in the navy; and one of them was Commodore George Dewey. Roosevelt had kept his eye on him for some time as an officer who "could be relied upon to prepare in advance, and to act promptly, fearlessly, and on his own responsibility when the emergency arose." When he began to foresee the probability of war, Roosevelt succeeded in having Dewey sent to command the Asiatic squadron; and just ten days after the Maine was blown up this cablegram went from Washington to Hong Kong:

"DEWEY, Hong Kong:

"Order the squadron, except the Monocacy, to Hong Kong. Keep full of coal. In the event of declaration of war Spain, your duty will be to see that the Spanish squadron does not leave the Asiatic coast, and then offensive operations in Philippine Islands. Keep Olympia until further orders. Roosevelt."

The declaration of war lagged on for nearly two months, but when it finally came, just one week elapsed between the sending of an order to Dewey to proceed at once to the Philippines and to "capture vessels or destroy" and the elimination of the sea power of Spain in the Orient. The battle of Manila Bay was a practical demonstration of the value of the "fighting edge," as exemplified in an Assistant

Secretary who fought procrastination, timidity, and political expedience at home and in a naval officer who fought the enemy's ships on the other side of the world.

When war actually came, Roosevelt could not stand inactivity in Washington. He was a fighter and he must go where the real fighting was. With Leonard Wood, then a surgeon in the army, he organized the First United States Volunteer Cavalry. He could have been appointed Colonel, but he knew that Wood knew more about the soldier's job than he, and he insisted upon taking the second place. The Secretary of War thought him foolish to step aside thus and suggested that Roosevelt become Colonel and Wood Lieutenant-Colonel, adding that Wood would do the work anyway. But that was not the Roosevelt way. He replied that he did not wish to rise on any man's shoulders, that he hoped to be given every chance that his deeds and his abilities warranted, that he did not wish what he did not earn, and that, above all, he did not wish to hold any position where any one else did the work. Lieutenant-Colonel he was made.

The regiment, which will always be affectionately known as the Rough Riders, was "raised, armed, equipped, drilled, mounted, dismounted, kept for two weeks on a transport, and then put through two victorious aggressive fights, in which it lost a third of the officers, and a fifth of the enlisted men, all within a little over fifty days." Roosevelt began as second in command, went through the battle of San Juan Hill as Colonel, and ended the war in command of a brigade, with the brevet of Brigadier-General. The title of Colonel stuck to him all his life.

When he became President, his instinctive commitment to the necessity of being prepared had been stoutly reinforced by his experience in what he called "the war of America the Unready." His first message to Congress was a long and exhaustive paper, dealing with many matters of importance. But almost one-fifth of it was devoted to the army and the navy. "It is not possible," he said, "to improvise a navy after war breaks out. The ships must be built and the men trained long in advance." He urged that Congress forthwith provide for several additional battleships and heavy armored cruisers, together with the proportionate number of smaller craft, and he pointed out the need for many more officers and men. He declared that "even in time of peace a warship should be used until it wears out, for only so can it be kept fit to respond to any emergency. The officers and men alike should be kept as much as possible on blue water, for it is there only they can learn their duties as they should be learned." But his most vigorous insistence was upon gunnery. "In battle," he said once to the graduates of the Naval Academy, "the only shots that count are those that hit, and marksmanship is a matter of long practice and intelligent reasoning." To this end he demanded "unceasing" gunnery practice.

In every succeeding message to Congress for seven years he returned to the subject of the navy, demanding ships, officers, men, and, above all, training. His insistence on these essentials brought results, and by the time the cruise of the battle fleet around the world had been achieved, the American navy, ship for ship, was not surpassed by any in the world. Perhaps it would be more accurate to say, ship's crew for ship's crew; for it was the officers and men of the American navy who made it possible for the world cruise to be made without the smallest casualty.

The question of marksmanship had been burned into Roosevelt's mind in those days when the Spanish War was brewing. He has related in his "Autobiography" how it first came to his attention through a man whose name has in more recent years become known the world over in connection with the greatest task of the American navy. Roosevelt's account is as follows:

"There was one deficiency... which there was no time to remedy, and of the very existence of which, strange to say, most of our best men were ignorant. Our navy had no idea how low our standard of marksmanship was. We had not realized that the modern battleship had become such a complicated piece of mechanism that the old methods of training in marksmanship were as obsolete as the old muzzle-loading broadside guns themselves. Almost the only man in the navy who fully realized this was our naval attach at Paris, Lieutenant Sims. He wrote letter after letter pointing out how frightfully backward we were in marksmanship. I was much impressed by his letters.... As Sims proved to be mistaken in his belief that the French had taught the Spaniards how to shoot, and as the Spaniards proved to be much worse even than we were, in the service generally Sims was treated as an alarmist. But although I at first partly acquiesced in this view, I grew uneasy when I studied the small proportion of hits to shots made by our vessels in battle. When I was President I took up the matter, and speedily became convinced that we needed to revolutionize our whole training in marksmanship. Sims was given the lead in organizing and introducing the new system; and to him more than to any other one man was due the astonishing progress made by our fleet in this respect, a progress which made the fleet, gun for gun, at least three times as effective, in point of fighting efficiency, in 1908, as it was in 1902".[9]

Theodore Roosevelt was a thoroughgoing, bred-in-the-bone individualist, but not as the term is ordinarily understood. He continually emphasized not the rights of the individual, but his duties, obligations, and opportunities. He knew that human character is the greatest thing in the world and that men and women are the real forces that move and sway the world's affairs. So in all his preaching and doing on behalf of a great and efficient navy, the emphasis that he always laid was upon the men of the navy, their efficiency and their spirit. He once remarked, "I believe in the navy of the United States primarily because I believe in the intelligence, the patriotism, and the fighting edge of the average man of the navy." To the graduating class at Annapolis, he once said:

"There is not one of you who is not derelict in his duty to the whole Nation if he fails to prepare himself with all the strength that in him lies to do his duty should the occasion arise; and one of your great duties is to see that shots hit. The result is going to depend largely upon whether you or your adversary hits. I expect you to be brave. I rather take that for granted.... But, in addition, you have got to prepare yourselves in advance. Every naval action that has taken place in the last twenty years ... has shown, as a rule, that the defeated party has suffered not from lack of courage, but because it could not make the best use of its weapons, or had not been given the right weapons... . I want every one here to proceed upon the assumption that any foe he may meet will have the courage. Of course, you have got to show the highest degree of courage yourself or you will be beaten anyhow, and you will deserve to be; but in addition to that you must prepare yourselves by careful training so that you may make the best possible use of the delicate and formidable mechanism of a modern warship."

Theodore Roosevelt was an apostle of preparedness from the hour that he began to think at all about affairs of public moment--and that hour came to him earlier in life than it does to most men. In the preface to his history of the War of 1812, which he wrote at the age of twenty-four, this sentence appears: "At present people are beginning to realize that it is folly for the great English-speaking Republic to rely for defense upon a navy composed partly of antiquated hulks, and partly of new vessels

---

9  Autobiography

rather more worthless than the old." His prime interest, from the point of view of preparedness, lay in the navy. His sense of proportion told him that the navy was the nation's first line of defense. He knew that without an efficient navy a nation situated as the United States was would be helpless before an aggressive enemy, and that, given a navy of sufficient size and effectiveness, the nation could dispense with a great army. For the army he demanded not size but merely efficiency. One of his principal points of attack in his criticism of the army was the system of promotion for officers. He assailed sharply the existing practice of "promotion by mere seniority." In one of his messages to Congress he pointed out that a system of promotion by merit existed in the Military Academy at West Point. He then went on to say that from the time of the graduation of the cadets into the army "all effort to find which man is best or worst and reward or punish him accordingly, is abandoned: no brilliancy, no amount of hard work, no eagerness in the performance of duty, can advance him, and no slackness or indifference, that falls short of a court-martial offense, can retard him. Until this system is changed we cannot hope that our officers will be of as high grade as we have a right to expect, considering the material from which we draw. Moreover, when a man renders such service as Captain Pershing rendered last spring in the Moro campaign, it ought to be possible to reward him without at once jumping him to the grade of brigadier-general."

It is not surprising to find in this message also a name that was later to become famous in the Great War. Roosevelt had an uncanny gift of prophecy.

More than once, as President, he picked out for appreciation and commendation the very men who were to do the big things for America when the critical hour came.

# CHAPTER XVI. THE LAST FOUR YEARS

When the Great War broke out in August, 1914, Roosevelt instantly stiffened to attention. He immediately began to read the lessons that were set for the world by the gigantic conflict across the sea and it was not long before he was passing them on to the American people. Like every other good citizen, he extended hearty support to the President in his conduct of America's foreign relations in the crisis. At the same time, however, he recognized the possibility that a time might come when it would be a higher moral duty to criticize the Administration than to continue unqualified support. Three weeks after war had begun, Roosevelt wrote in "The Outlook":

"In common with the immense majority of our fellow countrymen, I shall certainly stand by not only the public servants in control of the Administration at Washington, but also all other public servants, no matter of what party, during this crisis; asking only that they with wisdom and good faith endeavor to take every step that can be taken to safeguard the honor and interest of the United States, and, so far as the opportunity offers, to promote the cause of peace and justice throughout the world. My hope, of course, is that in their turn the public servants of the people will take no action so fraught with possible harm to the future of the people as to oblige farsighted and patriotic men to protest against it."

One month later, in a long article in "The Outlook", Roosevelt reiterated this view in these words:

".... We, all of us, without regard to party differences, must stand ready loyally to support the Administration, asking nothing except that the policy be one that in truth and in fact tells for the honor and interest of our Nation and in truth and in fact is helpful to the cause of a permanent and righteous world peace."

In the early months of the war, Roosevelt thus scrupulously endeavored to uphold the President's hands, to utter no criticism that might hamper him, and to carry out faithfully the President's adjuration to neutrality. He recognized clearly, however, the price that we must pay for neutrality, and he set it forth in the following passage from the same article: "A deputation of Belgians has arrived in this country to invoke our assistance in the time of their dreadful need. What action our Government can or will take I know not. It has been announced that no action can be taken that will interfere with our entire neutrality. It is certainly eminently desirable that we should remain entirely neutral, and nothing but urgent need would warrant breaking our neutrality and taking sides one way or the other. Our first duty is to hold ourselves ready to do whatever the changing circumstances demand in order to protect our own interests in the present and in the future; although, for my own part, I desire to add to this statement the proviso that under no circumstances must we do anything dishonorable, especially toward unoffending weaker nations. Neutrality may be of prime necessity in order to preserve our own interests, to maintain peace in so much of the world as is not affected by the war, and to conserve our influence for helping toward the reestablishment of general peace when the time comes; for if any outside Power is able at such time to be the medium for bringing peace, it is more likely to be the United States than any other. But we pay the penalty of this action on behalf of peace for ourselves, and possibly for others in the future, by forfeiting our right to do anything on behalf of peace for the Belgians in the present. We can maintain our neutrality only by refusal to do anything to aid unoffending weak powers which are dragged into the gulf of bloodshed and misery through no fault of their own. Of course it would be folly to jump into the gulf ourselves to no good purpose; and very probably nothing that we could have done would have helped Belgium. We have not the smallest responsibility for what has befallen her, and I am sure that the sympathy of this country for the men, women, and children of Belgium is very real. Nevertheless, this sympathy is compatible with full acknowledgment of the unwisdom of our uttering a single word of official protest unless we are prepared to make that protest effective; and only the clearest and most urgent national duty would ever justify us in deviating from our rule of neutrality and noninterference. But it is a grim comment on the professional pacifist theories as hitherto developed that our duty to preserve peace for ourselves may necessarily mean the abandonment of all effective efforts to secure peace for other unoffending nations which through no fault of their own are dragged into the War."

The rest of the article concerned itself with the lessons taught by the war, the folly of pacifism, the need for preparedness if righteousness is not to be sacrificed for peace, the worthlessness of treaties unsanctioned by force, and the desirability of an association of nations for the prevention of war. On this last point Roosevelt wrote as follows:

"But in view of what has occurred in this war, surely the time ought to be ripe for the nations to consider a great world agreement among all the civilized military powers TO BACK RIGHTEOUSNESS BY FORCE. Such an agreement would establish an efficient World League for the Peace of Righteousness. Such an agreement could limit the amount to be spent on armaments and, after defining carefully the inalienable rights of each nation which were not to be transgressed by any other, could also provide that any cause of difference among them, or between one of them and one of a certain number of designated outside non-military nations, should be submitted to an international court, including citizens of all these nations, chosen not as representatives of the nations, BUT AS JUDGES and perhaps in any given case the particular judges could be chosen by lot from the total number. To supplement and make this effectual it should be solemnly covenanted that if any nation refused to abide by the decision of such a court the others would draw the sword on behalf of peace and justice, and would unitedly coerce the recalcitrant nation. This plan would not automatically bring peace, and it may be too soon to hope for its adoption; but if some such scheme could be adopted, in good faith and with a genuine purpose behind it to make it effective, then we would have come nearer to the day of world peace. World peace will not come save in some such manner as that whereby we obtain peace within the borders of each nation; that is, by the creation of reasonably impartial judges and by putting an efficient police power-- that is, by putting force in efficient fashion--behind the decrees of the judges. At present each nation must in the last resort trust to its own strength if it is to preserve all that makes life worth having. At present this is imperative. This state of things can be abolished only when we put force, when we put the collective armed power of civilization, behind some body which shall with reasonable justice and equity represent the collective determination of civilization to do what is right."

From this beginning Roosevelt went on vigorously preaching preparedness against war; and the Great War had been raging for a scant seven months when he was irresistibly impelled to utter open criticism of President Wilson. In April, 1915, in The Metropolitan Magazine, to which he had transferred his writings, he declared that "the United States, thanks to Messrs. Wilson and Bryan, has signally failed in its duty toward Belgium." He maintained that the United States, under the obligations assumed by the signature of The Hague Conventions, should have protested to Germany against the invasion of Belgium.

For two years thereafter, while Germany slapped America first on one cheek and then on the other, and treacherously stabbed her with slinking spies and dishonored diplomats, Roosevelt preached, with growing indignation and vehemence, the cause of preparedness and national honor. He found it impossible to support the President further. In February, 1916, he wrote:

"Eighteen months have gone by since the Great War broke out. It needed no prescience, no remarkable statesmanship or gift of forecasting the future, to see that, when such mighty forces were unloosed, and when it had been shown that all treaties and other methods hitherto relied upon for national protection and for mitigating the horror and circumscribing the area of war were literally 'scraps of paper,' it had become a vital necessity that we should instantly and on a great and adequate scale prepare for our own defense. Our men, women, and children--not in isolated cases, but in scores and hundreds of cases--have been murdered by Germany and Mexico; and we have tamely submitted to wrongs from Germany and Mexico of a kind to which no nation can submit without impairing its own self-respect and incurring the contempt of the rest of mankind. Yet, during these eighteen months not one thing has been done.... Never in the country's history has there been a more stupendous instance of folly than this crowning folly of waiting eighteen months after the elemental crash of nations took place before even making a start in an effort--and an utterly inefficient and insufficient effort-for some kind of preparation to ward off disaster in the future.

"If President Wilson had shown the disinterested patriotism, courage, and foresight demanded by this stupendous crisis, I would have supported him with hearty enthusiasm. But his action, or rather inaction, has been such that it has become a matter of high patriotic duty to oppose him.... No man can support Mr. Wilson without at the same time supporting a policy of criminal inefficiency as regards the United States Navy, of short-sighted inadequacy as regards the army, of abandonment of the duty owed by the United States to weak and well-behaved nations, and of failure to insist on our just rights when we are ourselves maltreated by powerful and unscrupulous nations."

Theodore Roosevelt could not, without violating the integrity of his own soul, go on supporting either positively by word or negatively by silence the man who had said, on the day after the Lusitania was sunk, "There is such a thing as a nation being too proud to fight," and who later called for a "peace without victory." He could have nothing but scorn for an Administration whose Secretary of War could say, two months after the United States had actually entered the war, that there was "difficulty. ... disorder and confusion... in getting things started," and could then add, "but it is a happy confusion. I delight in the fact that when we entered this war we were not like our adversary, ready for it, anxious for it, prepared for it, and inviting it."

Until America entered the war Roosevelt used his voice and his pen with all his native energy and fire to convince the American people of three things that righteousness demanded that the United States forsake its supine neutrality and act; that the United States should prepare itself thoroughly for any emergency that might arise; and that the hyphenated Americanism of those who, while enjoying the benefits of American citizenship, "intrigue and conspire against the United States, and do their utmost to promote the success of Germany and to weaken the defense of this nation" should be rigorously curbed. The sermons that he preached on this triple theme were sorely needed. No leadership in this phase of national life was forthcoming from the quarter where the American people had every right to look for leadership. The White House had its face set in the opposite direction.

In August, 1915, an incident occurred which set the contrast between the Rooseveltian and Wilsonian lines of thought in bold relief. Largely through the initiative of General Leonard Wood there had been organized at Plattsburg, New York, an officers' training camp where American business men were given an all too brief course of training in the art and duty of leading soldiers in camp and in the field. General Wood was in command of the Plattsburg camp. He invited Roosevelt to address the men in training. Roosevelt accepted gladly, and in the course of his speech made these significant statements:

"For thirteen months America has played an ignoble part among the nations. We have tamely submitted to seeing the weak, whom we have covenanted to protect, wronged. We have seen our men, women, and children murdered on the high seas without protest. We have used elocution as a substitute for action.

"During this time our government has not taken the smallest step in the way of preparedness to defend our own rights. Yet these thirteen months have made evident the lamentable fact that force is more dominant now in the affairs of the world than ever before, that the most powerful of modern military nations is utterly brutal and ruthless in its disregard of international morality, and that righteousness divorced from force is utterly futile. Reliance upon high sounding words, unbacked by deeds, is proof of a mind that dwells only in the realm of shadow and of sham.

"It is not a lofty thing, on the contrary, it is an evil thing, to practise a timid and selfish neutrality between right and wrong. It is wrong for an individual. It is still more wrong for a nation.

"Therefore, friends, let us shape our conduct as a nation in accordance with the highest rules of international morality. Let us treat others justly and keep the engagements we have made, such as these in The Hague conventions, to secure just treatment for others. But let us remember that we shall be wholly unable to render service to others and wholly unable to fulfill the prime law of national being, the law of self-preservation, unless we are thoroughly prepared to hold our own. Let us show that a free democracy can defend itself successfully against any organized and aggressive military despotism."

The men in the camp heard him gladly and with enthusiasm. But the next day the Secretary of War sent a telegram of censure to General Wood in which he said:

"I have just seen the reports in the newspapers of the speech made by ex-President Roosevelt at the Plattsburg camp. It is difficult to conceive of anything which could have a more detrimental effect upon the real value of this experiment than such an incident.... No opportunity should have been furnished to any one to present to the men any matter excepting that which was essential to the necessary training they were to receive. Anything else could only have the effect of distracting attention from the real nature of the experiment, diverting consideration to issues which excite controversy, antagonism, and ill feeling and thereby impairing if not destroying, what otherwise would have been so effective."

On this telegram Roosevelt's comment was pungent: "If the Administration had displayed one-tenth the spirit and energy in holding Germany and Mexico to account for the murder of men, women, and children that it is now displaying in the endeavor to prevent our people from being taught the need of preparation to prevent the repetition of such murders in the future, it would be rendering a service to the people of the country."

Theodore Roosevelt could have little effect upon the material preparedness of the United States for the struggle which it was ultimately to enter. But he could and did have a powerful effect upon the spiritual preparedness of the American people for the efforts, the trials, and the sacrifices of that struggle. No voice was raised more persistently or more consistently than his. No personality was thrown with more power and more effect into the task of arousing the people of the United States to their duty to take part in the struggle against Prussianism. No man, in public or private life, urged so vigorously and effectively the call to arms against evil and for the right. His was the "voice crying in the wilderness," and to him the American spirit hearkened and awoke.

At last the moment came. Roosevelt had but one desire and one thought. He wanted to get to the firing-line. This was no impulse, no newly formed project. For two months he had been in correspondence with the Secretary of War on the subject. A year or more before that he had offered, in case America went into the war, to raise a volunteer force, train it, and take it across to the front. The idea was not new to him, even then. As far back as 1912 he had said on several different occasions, "If the United States should get into another war, I should raise a brigade of cavalry and lead it as I did my regiment in Cuba." It never occurred to him in those days that a former Commander-in-Chief of the United States Army, with actual experience in the field, would be refused permission to command troops in an American war. The idea would hardly have occurred to any one else. But that is precisely what happened.

On February 2, 1917, Roosevelt wrote to the Secretary of War reminding him that his application for permission to raise a division of infantry was already on file in the Department, saying that he was about to sail for Jamaica, and asking the

Secretary to inform him if he believed there would be war and a call for volunteers, for in that case he did not intend to sail. Secretary Baker replied, "No situation has arisen which would justify my suggesting a postponement of the trip you propose." Before this reply was received Roosevelt had written a second letter saying that, as the President had meanwhile broken off diplomatic relations with Germany, he should of course not sail. He renewed his request for permission to raise a division, and asked if a certain regular officer whom he would like to have for his divisional Chief of Staff, if the division were authorized, might be permitted to come to see him with a view to "making all preparations that are possible in advance." To this the Secretary replied, "No action in the direction suggested by you can be taken without the express sanction of Congress. Should the contingency Occur which you have in mind, it is to be expected that Congress will complete its legislation relating to volunteer forces and provide, under its own conditions, for the appointment of officers for the higher commands."

Roosevelt waited five weeks and then earnestly renewed his request. He declared his purpose to take his division, after some six weeks of preliminary training, direct to France for intensive training so that it could be sent to the front in the shortest possible time. Secretary Baker replied that no additional armies could be raised without the consent of Congress, that a plan for a much larger army was ready for the action of Congress when ever required, and that the general officers for all volunteer forces were to be drawn from the regular army. To this Roosevelt replied with the respectful suggestion that, as a retired Commander-in-Chief of the United States Army, he was eligible to any position of command over American troops. He recounted also his record of actual military experience and referred the Secretary to his immediate superiors in the field in Cuba as to his fitness for command of troops.

When war had been finally declared, Secretary Baker and Roosevelt conferred together at length about the matter. Thereafter Mr. Baker wrote definitely, declaring that he would be obliged to withhold his approval from an expedition of the sort proposed. The grounds which he gave for the decision were that the soldiers sent across must not be "deprived... of the most experienced leadership available, in deference to any mere sentimental consideration," and that it should appear from every aspect of the expeditionary force, if one should be sent over (a point not yet determined upon) that "military considerations alone had determined its composition."

To this definite refusal on the part of the Secretary of War Roosevelt replied at length. In his letter was a characteristic passage commenting upon Secretary Baker's reference to "sentimental considerations":

"I have not asked you to consider any "sentimental value" in this matter. I am speaking of moral effect, not of sentimental value. Sentimentality is as different from morality as Rousseau's life from Abraham Lincoln's. I have just received a letter from James Bryce urging "the dispatch of an American force to the theater of war," and saying, "The moral effect of the appearance in the war line of an American force would be immense." From representatives of the French and British Governments and of the French, British, and Canadian military authorities, I have received statements to the same effect, in even more emphatic form, and earnest hopes that I myself should be in the force. Apparently your military advisers in this matter seek to persuade you that a "military policy" has nothing to do with "moral effect." If so, their militarism is like that of the Aulic Council of Vienna in the Napoleonic Wars, and not like that of Napoleon, who stated that in war the moral was to the material as two to one. These advisers will do well to follow the teachings of Napoleon and not those of the pedantic militarists of the Aulic Council, who were the helpless victims of Napoleon."

Secretary Baker replied with a reiteration of his refusal. Roosevelt made one further attempt. When the Draft Law passed Congress, carrying with it the authorization to use volunteer forces, he telegraphed the President asking permission to raise two divisions, and four if so directed. The President replied with a definite negative, declaring that his conclusions were "based entirely upon imperative considerations of public policy and not upon personal or private choice." Meanwhile applications had been received from over three hundred thousand men desirous of joining Roosevelt's volunteer force, of whom it was estimated that at least two hundred thousand were physically fit, double the number needed for four divisions. That a single private citizen, by "one blast upon his bugle horn" should have been able to call forth three hundred thousand volunteers, all over draft age, was a tremendous testimony to his power. If his offer had been accepted when it was first made, there would have been an American force on the field in France long before one actually arrived there. It was widely believed, among men of intelligence and insight, not only in America but in Great Britain and France, that the arrival of such a force, under the command of a man known, admired, and loved the world over, would have been a splendid reinforcement to the Allied morale and a sudden blow to the German confidence. But the Administration would not have it so.

I shall never forget one evening with Theodore Roosevelt on a speaking tour which he was making through the South in 1912. There came to our private car for dinner Senator Clarke of Arkansas and Jack Greenway, young giant of football fame and experience with the Rough Riders in Cuba. After dinner, Jack, who like many giants, is one of the most diffident men alive, said hesitatingly:

"Colonel, I've long wanted to ask you something."

"Go right ahead," said T. R., "what is it?"

"Well, Colonel," said Jack, "I've always believed that it was your ambition to die on the field of battle."

T. R. brought his hand down on the table with a crash that must have hurt the wood.

"By Jove," said he, "how did you know that?"

"Well, Colonel," said Jack, "do you remember that day in Cuba, when you and I were going along a trail and came upon    [one of the regiment] propped against a tree, shot through the abdomen? It was evident that he was done for. But instead of commiserating him, you grabbed his hand and said something like this, 'Well, old man, isn't this splendid!' Ever since then I've been sure you would be glad to die in battle yourself."

T. R.'s face sobered a little.

"You're right, Jack," he said. "I would."

The end of Theodore Roosevelt's life seemed to come to him not in action but in quietness. But the truth was other than that. For it, let us turn again to Browning's lines:

> I was ever a fighter, so--one fight more,
> The best and the last!
> I would hate that death bandaged my eyes, and forbore,
> And bade me creep past.

On the fifth of January in 1919, after sixty years of life, full of unwearied fighting against evil and injustice and falseness, he "fell on sleep." The end came peacefully in the night hours at Sagamore Hill. But until he laid him down that night, the fight he waged had known no relaxation. Nine months before he had expected death, when a serious mastoid operation had drained his vital forces. Then his one thought had been, not for himself, but for his sons to whom had been given the precious privilege, denied to him, of taking part in their country's and the world's great fight for righteousness. His sister, Mrs. Corinne Douglas Robinson, tells how in those shadowy hours he beckoned her to him and in the frailest of whispers said, "I'm glad it's I that lie here and that my boys are in the fight over there."

His last, best fight was worthy of all the rest. With voice and pen he roused the minds and the hearts of his countrymen to their high mission in defense of human rights. It was not given to him to fall on the field of battle. But he went down with his face to the forces of evil with which he had never sought a truce.

# BIBLIOGRAPHICAL NOTE

The reader who is primarily interested in the career and personality of Roosevelt would do well to begin with his own volume, "Theodore Roosevelt, An Autobiography". But it was written in 1912, before the great campaign which produced the Progressive party.

"Theodore Roosevelt the Citizen" (1904), by Jacob A. Riis, was published just after Roosevelt became President. It is an intimate and naively enthusiastic portrait by a man who was an intimate friend and an ardent admirer.

There are two lives written since his death that are complete and discriminating. They are "The Life of Theodore Roosevelt" (1919), by William Draper Lewis, and "Theodore Roosevelt, an Intimate Biography" (1919), by William Roscoe Thayer.

"Impressions of Theodore Roosevelt" (1919) is a volume of first-hand experiences, written by Lawrence F. Abbott of "The Outlook". The author was closely associated with Roosevelt on "The Outlook"; and after the African hunting trip met him at Khartum and went with him on his tour of the capitals of Europe.

A small volume by Charles G. Washburn,"Theodore Roosevelt, the Logic of His Career" (1916), contains the interpretation of a long-time friend and sincere admirer.

Collections of Roosevelt's writings and speeches covering the years from his becoming Governor of New York to the end of his Presidential terms are found in "The Roosevelt Policy", 2 vols. (1908) and "Presidential Addresses and State Papers", 4 vols. (1904). "The New Nationalism" (1910) is a collection of his speeches delivered between his return from Africa and the beginning of the Progressive campaign. His writings and speeches during the Great War are found in several volumes: "America and the World War" (1915); "Fear God and Take Your Own Part"

(1916); "The Foes of Our Own Household" (1917); "The Great Adventure" (1919).

Material on the Progressive movement and the Progressive party are to be found in "The Progressive Movement" (1915), by Benjamin Parke De Witt, "The Progressive Movement, Its Principles and Its Programme" (1913), by S. J. Duncan-Clark, "Presidential Nominations and Elections" (1916), by Joseph Bucklin Bishop, and "Third Party Movements" (1916), by Fred E. Haynes. The story of La Follette is set forth at greater length in his "Autobiography; A Personal Narrative of Political Experiences" (1918). Three other autobiographies contribute to an understanding of politics: "The Autobiography of Thomas C. Platt" (1910); J. B. Foraker, "Notes of a Busy Life", 2 vols. (1916). S. M. Cullom, "Fifty Years of Public Service" (1911).

The history of the country during the years when Roosevelt became a national figure is recounted by J. H. Latane in "America as a World Power" and by F. A. Ogg in "National Progress", both volumes in the "American Nation" Series. Briefer summaries of the general history of at least a part of the period treated in the present volume are to be found in Frederic L. Paxson's "The New Nation" (1915), and Charles A. Beard's "Contemporary American History" (1914).

The prosecution of the trusts may be followed in "Trust Laws and Unfair Competition" (Government Printing Office, 1916). Much useful material is contained in "Trusts, Pools and Corporations", edited by W. Z. Ripley (1916). W. H. Taft in "The Anti-Trust Law and the Supreme Court" (1914) defends the Sherman Act as interpreted by the courts during his administration.

The progress of social and industrial justice is outlined in "Principles of Labor Legislation" (1916), by John R. Commons and John B. Andrews. The problems of conservation and the history of governmental policy are set forth by C. R. Van Hise in "The Conservation of Natural Resources in the United States" (1910).

The "American Year Book" for the years 1910 to 1919 and the "New International Year Book" for the years 1907 to 1919 are invaluable sources of accurate and comprehensive information on the current history of the United States for the period which they cover.

Willis Fletcher Johnson's "America's Foreign Relations", 2 vols. (1915) is a history of the relations of the United States to the rest of the world. A shorter account is given in C. R. Fish's "American Diplomacy" (1915).

But much of the best material for the historical study of the first decade and a half of the twentieth century is to be found in the pages of the magazines and periodicals published during those years. "The Outlook", "The Independent", "The Literary Digest", "Collier's", "The Review of Reviews", "The World's Work", "Current Opinion", "The Nation", "The Commoner", La Follette's "Weekly"--all these are sources of great value. The Outlook is of especial usefulness because of Mr. Roosevelt's connection with it as Contributing Editor during the years between 1909 and 1914.

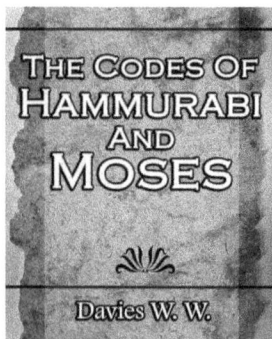

## The Codes Of Hammurabi And Moses
### W. W. Davies

QTY

The discovery of the Hammurabi Code is one of the greatest achievements of archaeology, and is of paramount interest, not only to the student of the Bible, but also to all those interested in ancient history...

Religion     **ISBN:** *1-59462-338-4*          **Pages:132**
                                                *MSRP $12.95*

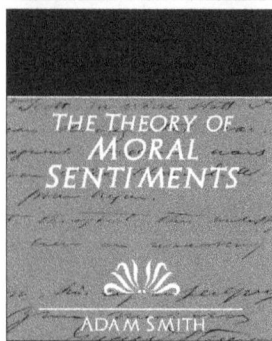

## The Theory of Moral Sentiments
### Adam Smith

QTY

This work from 1749. contains original theories of conscience amd moral judgment and it is the foundation for systemof morals.

Philosophy   **ISBN:** *1-59462-777-0*          **Pages:536**
                                                *MSRP $19.95*

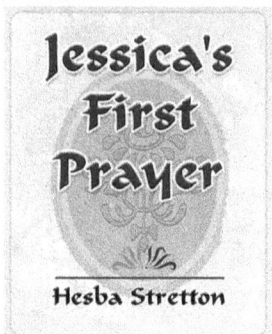

## Jessica's First Prayer
### Hesba Stretton

QTY

In a screened and secluded corner of one of the many railway-bridges which span the streets of London there could be seen a few years ago, from five o'clock every morning until half past eight, a tidily set-out coffee-stall, consisting of a trestle and board, upon which stood two large tin cans, with a small fire of charcoal burning under each so as to keep the coffee boiling during the early hours of the morning when the work-people were thronging into the city on their way to their daily toil...

Childrens    **ISBN:** *1-59462-373-2*          **Pages:84**
                                                *MSRP $9.95*

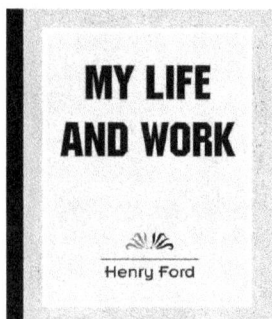

## My Life and Work
### Henry Ford

QTY

Henry Ford revolutionized the world with his implementation of mass production for the Model T automobile. Gain valuable business insight into his life and work with his own auto-biography... "We have only started on our development of our country we have not as yet, with all our talk of wonderful progress, done more than scratch the surface. The progress has been wonderful enough but..."

Biographies/ **ISBN:** *1-59462-198-5*          **Pages:300**
                                                *MSRP $21.95*

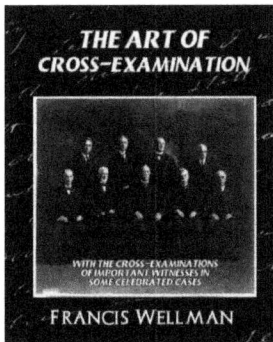

## The Art of Cross-Examination
## Francis Wellman

QTY

I presume it is the experience of every author, after his first book is published upon an important subject, to be almost overwhelmed with a wealth of ideas and illustrations which could readily have been included in his book, and which to his own mind, at least, seem to make a second edition inevitable. Such certainly was the case with me; and when the first edition had reached its sixth impression in five months, I rejoiced to learn that it seemed to my publishers that the book had met with a sufficiently favorable reception to justify a second and considerably enlarged edition. ..

**Pages:412**

Reference    ISBN: *1-59462-647-2*    *MSRP $19.95*

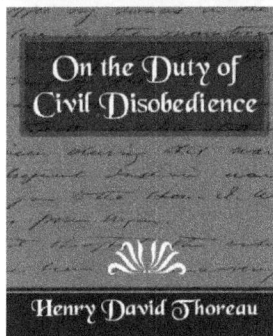

## On the Duty of Civil Disobedience
## Henry David Thoreau

QTY

Thoreau wrote his famous essay, On the Duty of Civil Disobedience, as a protest against an unjust but popular war and the immoral but popular institution of slave-owning. He did more than write—he declined to pay his taxes, and was hauled off to gaol in consequence. Who can say how much this refusal of his hastened the end of the war and of slavery ?

Law    ISBN: *1-59462-747-9*    **Pages:48**

*MSRP $7.45*

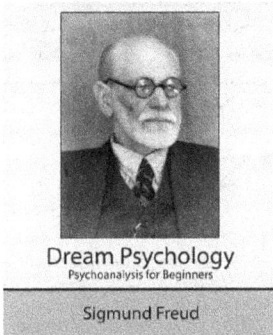

## Dream Psychology Psychoanalysis for Beginners
## Sigmund Freud

QTY

Sigmund Freud, born Sigismund Schlomo Freud (May 6, 1856 - September 23, 1939), was a Jewish-Austrian neurologist and psychiatrist who co-founded the psychoanalytic school of psychology. Freud is best known for his theories of the unconscious mind, especially involving the mechanism of repression; his redefinition of sexual desire as mobile and directed towards a wide variety of objects; and his therapeutic techniques, especially his understanding of transference in the therapeutic relationship and the presumed value of dreams as sources of insight into unconscious desires.

**Pages:196**

Psychology    ISBN: *1-59462-905-6*    *MSRP $15.45*

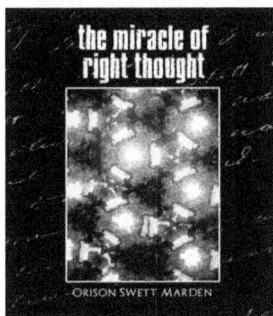

## The Miracle of Right Thought
## Orison Swett Marden

QTY

Believe with all of your heart that you will do what you were made to do. When the mind has once formed the habit of holding cheerful, happy, prosperous pictures, it will not be easy to form the opposite habit. It does not matter how improbable or how far away this realization may see, or how dark the prospects may be, if we visualize them as best we can, as vividly as possible, hold tenaciously to them and vigorously struggle to attain them, they will gradually become actualized, realized in the life. But a desire, a longing without endeavor, a yearning abandoned or held indifferently will vanish without realization.

**Pages:360**

Self Help    ISBN: *1-59462-644-8*    *MSRP $25.45*

**www.bookjungle.com** *email: sales@bookjungle.com fax: 630-214-0564 mail: Book Jungle  PO Box 2226  Champaign, IL 61825*

QTY

**The Rosicrucian Cosmo-Conception Mystic Christianity** *by Max Heindel*    ISBN: *1-59462-188-8*   **$38.95**
*The Rosicrucian Cosmo-conception is not dogmatic, neither does it appeal to any other authority than the reason of the student. It is: not controversial, but is: sent forth in the, hope that it may help to clear...*                                                         *New Age/Religion Pages 646*

**Abandonment To Divine Providence** *by Jean-Pierre de Caussade*    ISBN: *1-59462-228-0*   **$25.95**
*"The Rev. Jean Pierre de Caussade was one of the most remarkable spiritual writers of the Society of Jesus in France in the 18th Century. His death took place at Toulouse in 1751. His works have gone through many editions and have been republished...*         *Inspirational/Religion Pages 400*

**Mental Chemistry** *by Charles Haanel*    ISBN: *1-59462-192-6*   **$23.95**
*Mental Chemistry allows the change of material conditions by combining and appropriately utilizing the power of the mind.  Much like applied chemistry creates something new and unique out of careful combinations of chemicals the mastery of mental chemistry...*            *New Age Pages 354*

**The Letters of Robert Browning and Elizabeth Barret Barrett 1845-1846 vol II**    ISBN: *1-59462-193-4*   **$35.95**
*by Robert Browning and Elizabeth Barrett*
                                                                                                     *Biographies Pages 596*

**Gleanings In Genesis (volume I)** *by Arthur W. Pink*    ISBN: *1-59462-130-6*   **$27.45**
*Appropriately has Genesis been termed "the seed plot of the Bible" for in it we have, in germ form, almost all of the great doctrines which are afterwards fully developed in the books of Scripture which follow...*                                             *Religion/Inspirational Pages 420*

**The Master Key** *by L. W. de Laurence*    ISBN: *1-59462-001-6*   **$30.95**
*In no branch of human knowledge has there been a more lively increase of the spirit of research during the past few years than in the study of Psychology, Concentration and Mental Discipline. The requests for authentic lessons in Thought Control, Mental Discipline and...*    *New Age/Business Pages 422*

**The Lesser Key Of Solomon Goetia** *by L. W. de Laurence*    ISBN: *1-59462-092-X*   **$9.95**
*This translation of the first book of the "Lernegton" which is now for the first time made accessible to students of Talismanic Magic was done, after careful collation and edition, from numerous Ancient Manuscripts in Hebrew, Latin, and French...*             *New Age/Occult Pages 92*

**Rubaiyat Of Omar Khayyam** *by Edward Fitzgerald*    ISBN:*1-59462-332-5*   **$13.95**
*Edward Fitzgerald, whom the world has already learned, in spite of his own efforts to remain within the shadow of anonymity, to look upon as one of the rarest poets of the century, was born at Bredfield, in Suffolk, on the 31st of March, 1809. He was the third son of John Purcell...*   *Music Pages 172*

**Ancient Law** *by Henry Maine*    ISBN: *1-59462-128-4*   **$29.95**
*The chief object of the following pages is to indicate some of the earliest ideas of mankind, as they are reflected in Ancient Law, and to point out the relation of those ideas to modern thought.*                                                          *Religion/History Pages 452*

**Far-Away Stories** *by William J. Locke*    ISBN: *1-59462-129-2*   **$19.45**
*"Good wine needs no bush, but a collection of mixed vintages does. And this book is just such a collection. Some of the stories I do not want to remain buried for ever in the museum files of dead magazine-numbers an author's not unpardonable vanity..."*                 *Fiction Pages 272*

**Life of David Crockett** *by David Crockett*    ISBN: *1-59462-250-7*   **$27.45**
*"Colonel David Crockett was one of the most remarkable men of the times in which he lived. Born in humble life, but gifted with a strong will, an indomitable courage, and unremitting perseverance...*                                                  *Biographies/New Age Pages 424*

**Lip-Reading** *by Edward Nitchie*    ISBN: *1-59462-206-X*   **$25.95**
*Edward B. Nitchie, founder of the New York School for the Hard of Hearing, now the Nitchie School of Lip-Reading, Inc, wrote "LIP-READING Principles and Practice". The development and perfecting of this meritorious work on lip-reading was an undertaking...*            *How-to Pages 400*

**A Handbook of Suggestive Therapeutics, Applied Hypnotism, Psychic Science**    ISBN: *1-59462-214-0*   **$24.95**
*by Henry Munro*
                                                                         *Health/New Age/Health/Self-help Pages 376*

**A Doll's House: and Two Other Plays** *by Henrik Ibsen*    ISBN: *1-59462-112-8*   **$19.95**
*Henrik Ibsen created this classic when in revolutionary 1848 Rome.  Introducing some striking concepts in playwriting for the realist genre, this play has been studied the world over.*                                                            *Fiction/Classics/Plays 308*

**The Light of Asia** *by sir Edwin Arnold*    ISBN: *1-59462-204-3*   **$13.95**
*In this poetic masterpiece, Edwin Arnold describes the life and teachings of Buddha.  The man who was to become known as Buddha to the world was born as Prince Gautama of India but he rejected the worldly riches and abandoned the reigns of power when...*  *Religion/History/Biographies Pages 170*

**The Complete Works of Guy de Maupassant** *by Guy de Maupassant*    ISBN: *1-59462-157-8*   **$16.95**
*"For days and days, nights and nights, I had dreamed of that first kiss which was to consecrate our engagement, and I knew not on what spot I should put my lips..."*                                                                    *Fiction/Classics Pages 240*

**The Art of Cross-Examination** *by Francis L. Wellman*    ISBN: *1-59462-309-0*   **$26.95**
*Written by a renowned trial lawyer, Wellman imparts his experience and uses case studies to explain how to  use psychology to extract desired information through questioning.*                                                          *How-to/Science/Reference Pages 408*

**Answered or Unanswered?** *by Louisa Vaughan*    ISBN: *1-59462-248-5*   **$10.95**
*Miracles of Faith in China*                                                                          *Religion Pages 112*

**The Edinburgh Lectures on Mental Science (1909)** *by Thomas*    ISBN: *1-59462-008-3*   **$11.95**
*This book contains the substance of a course of lectures recently given by the writer in the Queen Street Hall, Edinburgh. Its purpose is to indicate the Natural Principles governing the relation between Mental Action and Material Conditions...*          *New Age/Psychology Pages 148*

**Ayesha** *by H. Rider Haggard*    ISBN: *1-59462-301-5*   **$24.95**
*Verily and indeed it is the unexpected that happens! Probably if there was one person upon the earth from whom the Editor of this, and of a certain previous history, did not expect to hear again...*                                                     *Classics Pages 380*

**Ayala's Angel** *by Anthony Trollope*    ISBN: *1-59462-352-X*   **$29.95**
*The two girls were both pretty, but Lucy who was twenty-one who supposed to be simple and comparatively unattractive, whereas Ayala was credited, as her Bombwhat romantic name might show, with poetic charm and a taste for romance. Ayala when her father died was nineteen...*    *Fiction Pages 484*

**The American Commonwealth** *by James Bryce*    ISBN: *1-59462-286-8*   **$34.45**
*An interpretation of American democratic political theory.  It examines political mechanics and society from the perspective of Scotsman James Bryce*                                                                                 *Politics Pages 572*

**Stories of the Pilgrims** *by Margaret P. Pumphrey*    ISBN: *1-59462-116-0*   **$17.95**
*This book explores pilgrims religious oppression in England as well as their escape to Holland and eventual crossing to America on the Mayflower, and their early days in New England...*                                                        *History Pages 268*

www.bookjungle.com *email: sales@bookjungle.com fax: 630-214-0564 mail: Book Jungle  PO Box 2226  Champaign, IL 61825*

QTY

**The Fasting Cure** by *Sinclair Upton*                                          ISBN: *1-59462-222-1*   **$13.95**
*In the Cosmopolitan Magazine for May, 1910, and in the Contemporary Review (London) for April, 1910, I published an article dealing with my experi-
ences in fasting. I have written a great many magazine articles, but never one which attracted so much attention...  New Age/Self Help/Health Pages 164*

**Hebrew Astrology** by *Sepharial*                                               ISBN: *1-59462-308-2*   **$13.45**
*In these days of advanced thinking it is a matter of common observation that we have left many of the old landmarks behind and that we are now pressing
forward to greater heights and to a wider horizon than that which represented the mind-content of our progenitors...          Astrology Pages 144*

**Thought Vibration or The Law of Attraction in the Thought World**              ISBN: *1-59462-127-6*   **$12.95**

by *William Walker Atkinson*                                                     *Psychology/Religion Pages 144*

**Optimism** by *Helen Keller*                                                    ISBN: *1-59462-108-X*   **$15.95**
*Helen Keller was blind, deaf, and mute since 19 months old, yet famously learned how to overcome these handicaps, communicate with the world, and
spread her lectures promoting optimism.  An inspiring read for everyone...                      Biographies/Inspirational Pages 84*

**Sara Crewe** by *Frances Burnett*                                               ISBN: *1-59462-360-0*    **$9.45**
*In the first place, Miss Minchin lived in London. Her home was a large, dull, tall one, in a large, dull square, where all the houses were alike, and all the
sparrows were alike, and where all the door-knockers made the same heavy sound...                Childrens/Classic Pages 88*

**The Autobiography of Benjamin Franklin** by *Benjamin Franklin*                ISBN: *1-59462-135-7*   **$24.95**
*The Autobiography of Benjamin Franklin has probably been more extensively read than any other American historical work, and no other book of its kind
has had such ups and downs of fortune. Franklin lived for many years in England, where he was agent...          Biographies/History Pages 332*

| Name | |
|------|---|
| Email | |
| Telephone | |
| Address | |
| | |
| City, State ZIP | |

☐ **Credit Card**              ☐ **Check / Money Order**

| Credit Card Number | |
|--------------------|---|
| Expiration Date | |
| Signature | |

*Please Mail to:  Book Jungle
PO Box 2226
Champaign, IL 61825
or Fax to:          630-214-0564*

## ORDERING INFORMATION

**web**: *www.bookjungle.com*
**email**: *sales@bookjungle.com*
**fax**: *630-214-0564*
**mail**: *Book Jungle  PO Box 2226  Champaign, IL 61825*
**or PayPal** *to sales@bookjungle.com*

*Please contact us for bulk discounts*

## DIRECT-ORDER TERMS

**20% Discount if You Order
Two or More Books**
Free Domestic Shipping!
Accepted: Master Card, Visa,
Discover, American Express